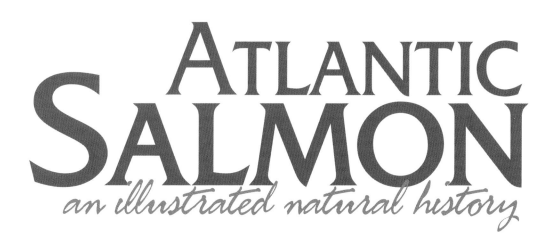

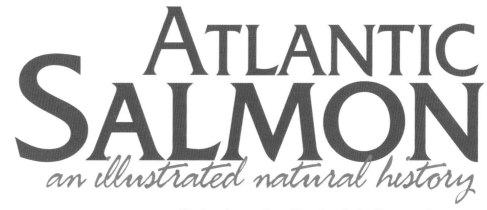

ATLANTIC
SALMON
an illustrated natural history

Paintings by Roderick Sutterby

Words by Malcolm Greenhalgh

Merlin Unwin Books

First published in Great Britain by Merlin Unwin Books, 2005

Paintings and illustrations copyright © Roderick Sutterby, 2005
Text copyright © Malcolm Greenhalgh, 2005

MERLIN UNWIN BOOKS
7 Corve Street, Ludlow
Shropshire SY8 1DB, U.K.
Tel 01584 877456
Fax 01584 877457

email: books@merlinunwin.co.uk
website: www.countrybooksdirect.com

British Library Cataloguing in Publication Data:
A catalogue record for this book is available from the British Library

ISBN 1-873674-73-2

Design www:thinkgraphicdesign.co.uk
Printed in Singapore by Star Standard Industries (Pte) Ltd

This book has been generously supported by
Fondation d'entreprise TOTAL for biodiversity and the sea

Contents

List of paintings and illustrations by Roderick Sutterby

Foreword

The 2004 season brought large numbers of Atlantic salmon to a great many salmon rivers. I believe it was the result of all the NASF-style agreements that now protect so much of the wild salmon's Atlantic range. This policy – of paying commercial fishermen to stop netting salmon – is the simplest and most effective way of putting more spawners into the rivers. We must wait to see whether this upsurge of returning fish is repeated in 2005. What is clear, however, from the failure of Ireland and Norway to share in this transformation, is that salmon stocks are now much stronger in regions where mixed-stock commercial fishing is no longer practised.

Those who still support salmon drift netting should read this book. Dr Malcolm Greenhalgh is such a distinguished piscatorial academic and writer that he deserves their attention. The rest of us will find he has surpassed himself in this new work and its impact is greatly enhanced by the beautiful paintings of artist Roderick Sutterby, also keen angler and naturalist.

We all imagine we know a great deal about our quarry. This fascinating exposition of the lifecycle of the salmon will make every reader realise that there is so much more to know. Packed with all the latest scientific knowledge it weaves hard facts so cleverly into the fabric of an enthralling narrative that I found it difficult to put down. I commend it to everyone who loves the King of Fish, the Atlantic salmon.

Orri Vigfússon
Chairman, North Atlantic Salmon Fund

'For by cause that the Samon is the moost stately fyssh that ony man maye angle to in fresshe water. Therfore I purpose to begyn at hym. The samon is a gentyll fysshe: but he is comborous for to take. For comynly he is but in depe places of grete ryures. And for the more parte he holdyth the myddys of it: that a man maye not come at hym.'

Dame Juliana Berners (attributed), *Treatyse of Fysshynge wyth an Angle,* 1496.

Introduction

I make no apologies for introducing yet another book about the Atlantic salmon. But before I continue, let me stress that this is not a book about catching salmon. There are, perhaps, too many of them. This book is simply about salmon.

It is a fact that no species of fish has had so much time, effort and money spent on researching its life story. Countries like Canada, France, Ireland, Scotland and Norway have government-funded laboratories studying salmon. Many university zoology or biological science departments have units investigating the salmon's ecology. By Act of Parliament each of the Environment Agency regions in England and Wales has the monitoring and improvement of salmon stocks as a priority. On a narrower but vitally important front, many individual rivers – such as the Loire in France, the Foyle and Bush in Ireland, the Tweed in Scotland and the Ribble and Eden in England – have their own conservation bodies. On the broadest front, national and international organisations are fighting to ensure the future of Atlantic salmon. In the British Isles there is The Salmon & Trout Association; on the European side of the Atlantic, The Atlantic Salmon Trust; and on the North American side, The Atlantic Salmon Federation; and, acting to control exploitation of salmon stocks, The North Atlantic Salmon Fund. Indeed, I will confidently modify the first sentence of this paragraph to say that no other wild creature on this planet has attracted so much funding and research as the Atlantic salmon.

However, this colossal effort affects not only the salmon. They need the cleanest of rivers if they are to survive. So, by striving to improve riverine conditions for the salmon, we also improve the lot of every other creature that depends on clean water. Salmon also need a productive North Atlantic Ocean. We now know that the quality of feeding for salmon (and many other North Atlantic fish) drastically declined in the third quarter of the twentieth century. As our understanding increases of how environmental conditions far out at sea affect the salmon and the creatures on which it feeds, we come, perhaps, a little closer to finding possible solutions to the problem.

Fascination with the salmon comes from more than its culinary, sporting and ecological interest. It is a beautiful fish. It is a powerful fish. It is an enigmatic fish with a most remarkable life history that we still do not fully comprehend. That is why this book has been produced; to celebrate the magnificent salmon, through paintings and words.

Malcolm Greenhalgh, Lowton, Lancashire

> *'Izaak [Walton] never wrote a true word about salmon except by accident – yet even today we find honest Izaak's silly speculations with scores of others sillier still, quoted and plagiarised by successive generations of compilers and ready-writers till the merest rubbish well-nigh acquires the sanctity of Holy Writ. Thus has the bibliography of the salmon reached the amazing total of 3000 volumes!'*
>
> Abel Chapman,
> *The Borders and Beyond*, 1924.

CHAPTER ONE

THE ATLANTIC SALMON

As Izaak Walton said of the Pike, it is "too good for any but anglers or honest men."

Hugh Falkus, speaking of the salmon as a gourmet food in the film *Salmo the Leaper* (BBC, *The World About Us* series, 1977)

There is no sight more beautiful than a fresh-run, wild, silver salmon. Its life cycle is a piece of magical natural history. On the table it is the epicurean's delight. Yet in recent years the reputation of the Atlantic salmon has been tarnished.

Today the salmon is one of the cheapest of culinary fish. Supermarkets stack their shelves with canned 'red', 'mid-red', 'pink' and 'sockeye' salmon imported from the Pacific coast of the USA and Canada. Farmed Atlantic salmon, from cages in Norwegian fjords, Scottish sea-lochs and – increasingly – the cool seas of southern Chile, is so abundant and inexpensive that it is consumed year-round in vast amounts. Despite health scares over the chemicals involved in its production, it is so ridiculously cheap that it is eaten in restaurants and bought from fish stalls all over the world. One fish-and-chip shop in Lerwick tried to sell me a slab of battered salmon from a local fish farm. It was half the price of haddock trawled from the surrounding Shetland seas. Recently, a Fuerteventuran restaurant had 'fresh' farmed salmon on the menu at a third of the price of locally-caught fresh snapper.

This superabundance of recent times has rather devalued the Atlantic salmon as a food fish in the eyes of many consumers. Before the 1980s, only those lucky enough to live close to salmon rivers, or wealthy visiting sportsmen, were in a position to enjoy eating the wild salmon that they or their acquaintances had caught themselves. Wild salmon were (and still are

in some places) harvested by netsmen whose catches were whisked off to markets to make a handsome profit. In the second half of the twentieth century, a train might leave Londonderry in Northern Ireland carrying the day's catch from the River Foyle to the ferry at Larne. By the next morning, it would be on sale in London's Billingsgate market at a premium price, intended for the luxury market. Prices then were far higher than the current going rate of perhaps under £2 per pound for farmed salmon that we see today.

It is vitally important, however, that we treat the wild salmon and farmed salmon as though they are different fish. Farmed salmon have ragged fins and scarred snouts, damaged by the cage-nets and by jostling for food among the seething mass of their peers. Their pink flesh colouration is largely chemically induced. Chemicals are also used to control pests and diseases that proliferate in the close confines of the fish cages.

Genetically, farmed salmon are subtly different from their wild cousins, having been bred for rapid growth rates and a certain tameness required for their overcrowded, caged existence. The farmed salmon on the fishmonger's slab is a caricature of what a salmon should be. It is like comparing a battery chicken with a proud Old English gamecock, crowing loudly from the top of its midden, king of all he surveys.

The wild Atlantic salmon is the true King of Fish.

A group of sea-silver salmon. It is only just before and during the marine phase of their lives that salmon are found in shoals or schools. Salmon often move at night

The King of Fish

Until its life history was worked out and most of its oceanic feeding grounds mapped, late in the twentieth century, the salmon was a creature of mystery. No other fish has so many distinct stages in its life: egg, alevin, fry, parr, smolt, post-smolt, grilse, salmon and kelt. Even today, the arrival of salmon back into the river from their ocean sojourn is a source of wonderment. Yesterday there were no fish in the pool, but today there are salmon leaping about everywhere. Where have they been? Why do they choose to run the river when they do? Why do some return after only one year at sea, while others may remain out at sea for two, three, or even four years? One cannot ask such complex questions about other fish whose life histories are so much simpler.

Besides its culinary value and its amazing life cycle, the salmon has another outstanding virtue. With its beauty, size and strength, added to its table appeal, the Atlantic salmon is highly prized by anglers. It is, perhaps, the quintessential fisherman's quarry and for many anglers it is the 'King' of all fish.

When I go fishing for pike I use a small dead fish, or lures that imitate small fish, because pike eat smaller fish. If I seek to catch carp, I might use an earthworm as bait, because carp like to eat earthworms. When I flyfish for brown trout and grayling, I use artificial flies tied with fur and feather to imitate the natural insects that these fish feed on. And so it is in most cases. The angler finds out what a particular fish habitually eats and puts that (or an imitation) on his hook. But this formula does not apply to salmon. As we shall see later (page 100), salmon do not feed when they return to their natal rivers to spawn.

Salmon angling is thus in a category of its own, completely lacking in logic. We tie what we call a 'fly' to our line, but this 'fly' usually looks like nothing that has ever lived. Then we cast our fly with an irrational hope that this splendid King of Fish (which gave up eating on its return to the river) might deign to take our offering.

Summer fish from the River Coquet, Northumberland, England. The head and shoulders of a salmon are perfectly-streamlined. When powered by sudden side-to-side thrusts of the tail, they allow for rapid acceleration, perhaps to flee from danger or to seize prey

Salmo the Leaper

'Because many of the Waters of Scotland are full of waterfalls, as soon as they come to a fall they leap.'

Hector Boase, *History of Scotland*, 1527

The scientific name of the Atlantic salmon is *Salmo salar*. Both generic and specific names derive from the Latin verb *salire*, which means 'to leap'. Leaping salmon must surely have been observed since prehistoric times by humans living near to tumbling salmon rivers.

The highest vertical waterfall which salmon have been observed leaping successfully is the Orrin Falls, on the River Orrin in Scotland. It is 11′ 4″ (3.4 metres) high. About five percent of the leaps observed here are successful, suggesting that the average fish makes about twenty attempts before succeeding.

People have long wondered at the leaping salmon and come up with many theories as to how it leaps. One very old idea was that a leaping salmon held its tail in its mouth, thus creating a wheel, and that the downfall of water caused this salmon-wheel to turn in such a way that it rolled up the outer face of the waterfall. Those promulgating this particular theory had clearly never watched leaping salmon! In his poem *Polyolbion* (1612), Michael Drayton took the tail-in-the-mouth theory a step further:

His tail takes in his mouth, and, bending like a bow
That's to full compass drawn, aloft doth throw.
Then springing at his height, as doth a little wand,
That, bended end to end, and started from man's hand,
Far off doth cast; so does the salmon vault.

So the leap is like a springy stick with the two ends held together, pointed up the waterfall and suddenly released. But that too is incorrect.

If you look at the surface of a plunge-pool at the foot of a waterfall you will see a stationary bulge in the surface of the pool a short distance from the bottom of the fall. This bulge is known as a 'standing wave'. The standing wave is the salmon's springboard. In attempting to leap a waterfall, the salmon accelerates to the water's surface and gives a final explosive thrust with its tail as it emerges through the standing wave. Once airborne, any further movement by the salmon will not add any extra height to the leap, but vigorous flapping of the tail helps the fish make it through the swift water at the lip of the fall into easier water beyond.

It appears that this standing wave can be quite critical in allowing the salmon to leap up high waterfalls successfully. Previously passable waterfalls have been rendered impassable when large boulders or other obstructions have fallen into the plunge-pool, thereby disrupting the formation of the standing wave. Impassable falls can sometimes be made passable by clearing boulders or tree debris from the plunge-pool.

A salmon expends much energy leaping a waterfall or forging its way upstream through fast water. That energy comes form reserves stored in its body when far out at sea on its marine feeding-grounds

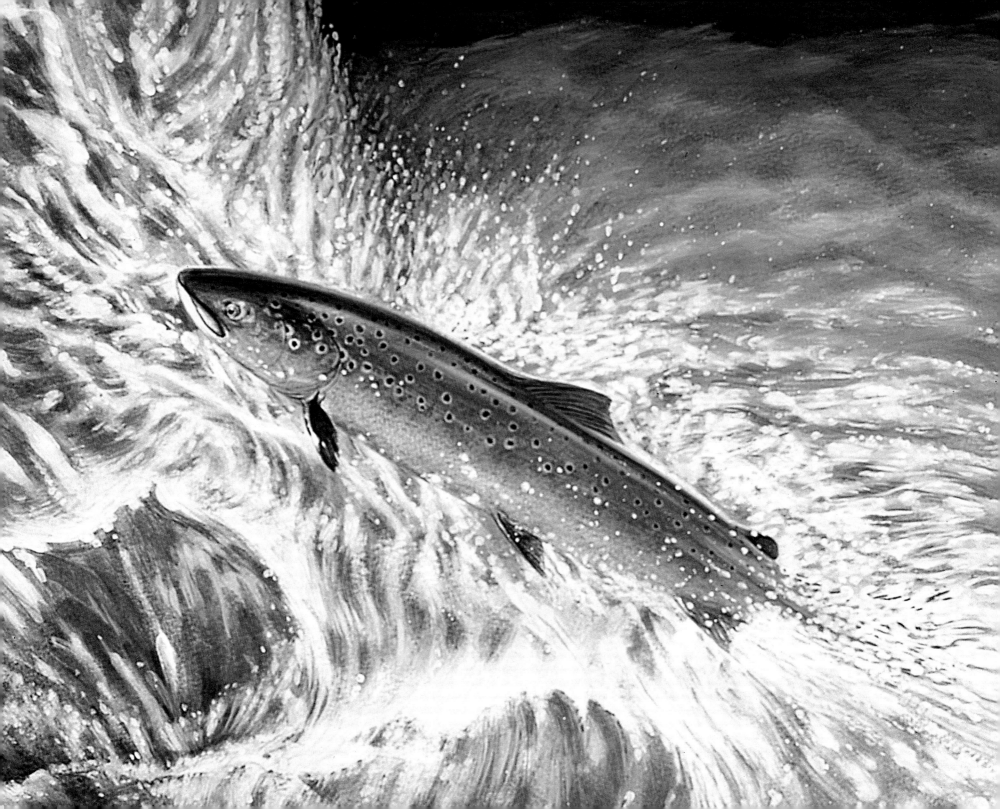

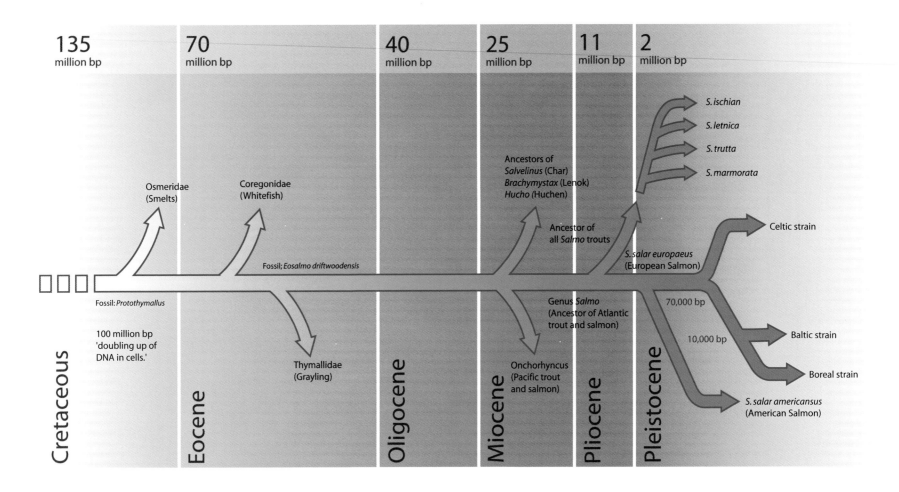

70 million bp

40 million bp

25 million bp

11 million bp

2 million bp

S. ischian

S. letnica

S. trutta

S. marmorata

Osmeridae (Smelts)

Coregonidae (Whitefish)

Ancestors of
Salvelinus (Char)
Brachymystax (Lenok)
Hucho (Huchen)

Ancestor of
all Salmo trouts

Celtic strain

S. salar europaeus
(European Salmon)

Fossil: Eosalmo driftwoodensis

Fossil: Protothymallus

Genus Salmo
(Ancestor of Atlantic
trout and salmon)

70,000 bp

10,000 bp

Baltic strain

100 million bp
'doubling up of
DNA in cells.'

Thymallidae
(Grayling)

Onchorhyncus
(Pacific trout
and salmon)

Boreal strain

S. salar americansus
(American Salmon)

Cretaceous

Eocene

Oligocene

Miocene

Pliocene

Pleistocene

The Family Tree of the Salmon

The greatest problem facing those wishing to trace the evolutionary development of river fish is that there simply isn't much of a fossil record. Instead of being buried in bottom sediments that eventually petrify their remains as fossils, the bodies of dead river fish tend to be eaten by scavengers, or are physically destroyed by the action of running water, or otherwise fail to find suitable conditions for fossilization. The evolutionary line leading to *Salmo salar* can best be deduced by comparing the structural and biochemical features of existing species, and linking them to our knowledge of events over geological time.

The roots of the salmon's family tree go back about 100 million years. when a close relation of the smelt (Family Osmeridae) suddenly doubled the genetic material (DNA) in its cells. This smelt relative eventually gave rise to the modern salmonids. Smelts do resemble small silvery salmonids, but they lack the axillary process (a pointed flap above the base of the pelvic fin) found in all fish higher up on the family tree, and they have an incomplete lateral line (which is complete in all others).

Whitefish (Family Coregonidae) were probably the next to leave the salmon's lineage, about 70 million years ago. Members of this family have,

like the smelts, large scales, but unlike the smelts are toothless or have minute teeth. A key feature of whitefish species is that, like the smelts, they scatter their eggs on the bottom of lake or river, whereas all others higher up the family tree cover their eggs in a gravel nest.

The grayling line (Family Thymallidae) branched away about 60 million years ago and probably evolved in a purely freshwater environment, for members of this family are the only ones in the salmon's family tree that cannot survive in sea water. Like the smelts, graylings have large scales, but they have minute teeth, a distinctly under-slung mouth

> 'New species have appeared very slowly, one after another, both on the land and in the waters.'
> Charles Darwin, *The Origin of Species*, 1859

and a huge dorsal fin in which the fin base length is greater than the length of the head.

One of the earliest predecessors of the salmon – a fossil of *Eosalmo driftwoodensis* – can be dated to about 60 million years ago. The Family Salmonidae evolved into the salmonids we see today.

About 25 million years ago, a branch separated from the main trunk and gave rise to three genera: the huchen (Hucho), the lenok (Brachymystax) and the chars (Salvelinus). The main stem of the tree thereafter leads to all modern trout and salmon.

The next major split occurred about 20 million years ago when the ancestors of the Atlantic basin trout and salmon became separated from their distant cousins in the Pacific basin. We therefore now have members of the genus Onchorhynchus living in rivers and lakes draining the Pacific shores, from Mexico north to Alaska and from the Chukot and Koryak mountain ranges of eastern Asiatic Siberia south to the Japanese archipelago. Members of the genus Salmo are found in rivers and lakes draining to the Atlantic and Mediterranean, from the High Arctic south to the Atlas Mountains of North Africa on the east, and Long Island Sound on the west.

The ancestors of the Salmo salmon and Salmo trout separated about 10 million years ago (though some researchers believe that the split occurred more recently, at 2-5 million years ago). It is likely that the distinct 'marbled trout' (*Salmo marmoratus*) separated from the Salmo trout line about two million years ago, leaving that line to produce the modern brown/sea trout (*Salmo trutta*). It is possible that two other species of trout split from the brown trout line in the past 100,000 years: *Salmo ischian* (now known only from Lake Sevan in Armenia)

and *Salmo letnica* (Lake Ohrid, Macedonia). Many, however, consider these to be merely subspecies of *Salmo trutta*.

So it seems that the Atlantic salmon *Salmo salar* is at most 10 million years old. But evolution has continued since then. Probably about 600,000 years ago the American population of the salmon became isolated from the European population sufficiently for the populations to warrant subspecies status: *Salmo salar americanus* and *Salmo salar europaeus*. Later, probably in the last Ice Age of 70,000-10,000 years ago, the European subspecies became split into two distinct genetic strains: the Celtic Strain to the south-west (which survived the last Ice Age in a glacial refuge in Iberia) and the Boreal Strain to the north-east (that survived the Ice Age in an ice-free lake in what is now the North Sea basin). After the end of the Ice Age, each population spread; the Celtic Strain northwards through northern France, the British Isles and southern Scandinavia; the Boreal Strain to Iceland, northern Scandinavia and Russia. Recent genetic-fingerprinting has traced interbreeding between the Celtic and Boreal Strains

Eosalmo driftwoodensis, a large-mouthed ancestor of the salmon which lived 60 million years ago. This image is made from a reconstruction from fossil records. The fish is large mouthed and deep bodied with a dorsal fin resembling the grayling

in northern France, eastern Britain and Fenno-Scandia; while the salmon of the Kola Peninsula are the only salmon of Europe to contain genetic traces of the North American population. Since the end of the last Ice Age, the population of the Boreal Strain living in the Baltic Sea became genetically distinct – a consequence of Baltic salmon rarely straying out to the Atlantic and interbreeding with Boreal Atlantic fish.

So the salmon continues to evolve – slowly.

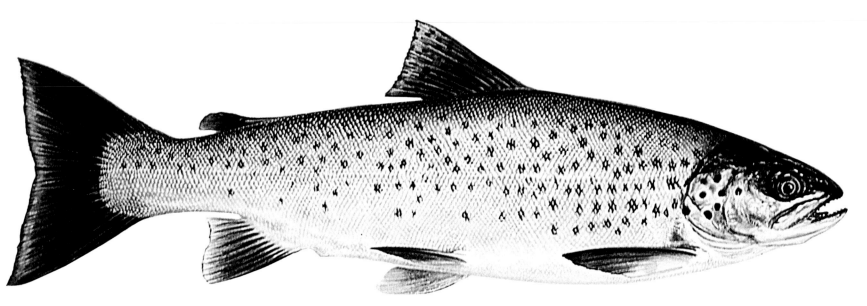

Brown trout from Scotland's Loch Leven. These lack the red spots found on most brown trout. The Leven strain of trout has been introduced into cool lakes and rivers throughout the world

Four Relations of the Salmon

Brown Trout

Salmo trutta The closest relation of the Atlantic salmon which can, in its silver sea-run form (sea trout), easily be mistaken for the salmon. Key anatomical features are: a jaw that extends well beyond the rear margin of the eye (only as far as the rear margin of the eye in salmon); 13-16 scales between the rear edge of the adipose fin and the lateral line (usually 11, occasionally 10-13 in salmon); when extended the rear edge of the tail fin is square or slightly convex in adult trout, forked in salmon.

Sockeye Salmon

Onchorhynchus nerka As in all members of this Pacific trout and salmon genus, the very long anal fin (with more than 12 branched rays; fewer in Salmo) and the very long jaws extending back well beyond the rear of the eye are diagnostic. Most species assume quite gaudy colours prior to spawning.

The Sockeye Salmon, despite several attempts, has never been successfully introduced to Atlantic rivers. This hen fish was from the Kern River, British Columbia

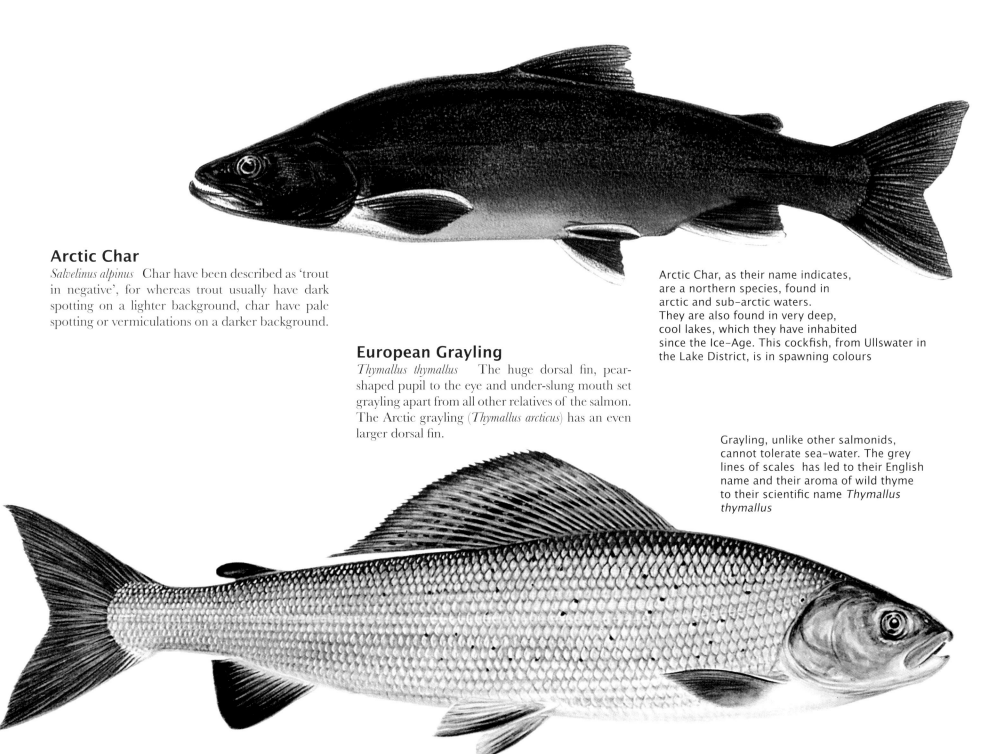

Arctic Char

Salvelinus alpinus Char have been described as 'trout in negative', for whereas trout usually have dark spotting on a lighter background, char have pale spotting or vermiculations on a darker background.

Arctic Char, as their name indicates, are a northern species, found in arctic and sub-arctic waters. They are also found in very deep, cool lakes, which they have inhabited since the Ice-Age. This cockfish, from Ullswater in the Lake District, is in spawning colours

European Grayling

Thymallus thymallus The huge dorsal fin, pear-shaped pupil to the eye and under-slung mouth set grayling apart from all other relatives of the salmon. The Arctic grayling (*Thymallus arcticus*) has an even larger dorsal fin.

Grayling, unlike other salmonids, cannot tolerate sea-water. The grey lines of scales has led to their English name and their aroma of wild thyme to their scientific name *Thymallus thymallus*

The Chief Members of the Salmon Family: Salmonidae

The Cherry salmon (*Onchorhynchus masu*) is from Japan. Note the distinctive 'parr' markings. The silver colouring indicates a migratory fish

Genus Salmo: Atlantic salmon (*Salmo salar*), brown trout/seatrout (*Salmo trutta*), Marbled trout (*Salmo marmoratus*)

Genus Onchorhynchus: pink salmon (*Onchorhynchus gorbuscha*), chinook or king salmon (*Onchorhynchus tsawytscha*), coho (*Onchorhynchus kisutch*), sockeye (*Onchorhynchus nerka*), chum salmon (*Onchorhynchus keta*), cherry salmon (*Onchorhynchus masou*), rainbow trout/steelhead (*Onchorhynchus mykiss*), cut-throat trout (*Onchorhynchus clarki*), Mexican golden trout (*Onchorhynchus chrysogaster*), Californian golden trout (*Onchorhynchus aguabonita*), gila/Apache trout (*Onchorhynchus gilae*)

Genus Salvelinus: Arctic char (*Salvelinus alpinus*), lake char (or lake trout) (*Salvelinus namaycush*), brook char (or brook trout) (*Salvelinus fontinalis*), dolly varden (*Salvelinus malma*), bull char (*Salvelinus confluentus*), stone char (*Salvelinus albus*), eastern char (*Salvelinus leucomaenis*)
N.B. This is a very controversial genus and many more Salvelinus species may eventually be recognised by taxonomists.

Genus Brachymystax: lenok (*Brachymystax lenok*)

Genus Hucho: huchen/taimen (*Hucho hucho*). *Hucho perryi* has no English name.

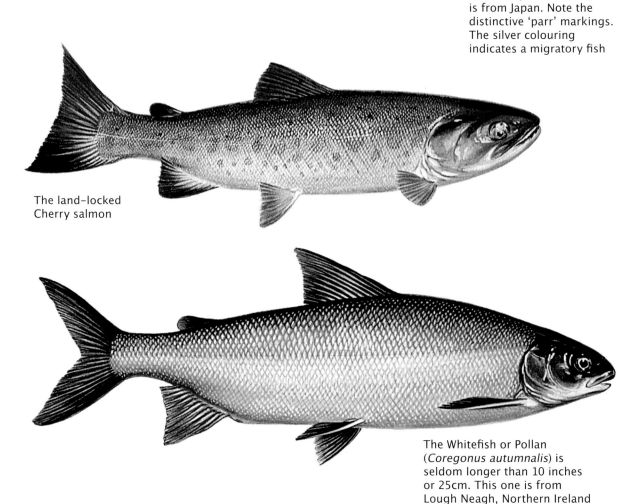

The land–locked Cherry salmon

The Whitefish or Pollan (*Coregonus autumnalis*) is seldom longer than 10 inches or 25cm. This one is from Lough Neagh, Northern Ireland

When Europeans first penetrated the North American continent, they quite naturally gave the animals they encountered, that resembled animals from back home, the same names. So it was that a thrush with brick-red breast was named the American robin (though it is not a close relation of the European robin) and a small, trout-like fish that they found in streams became the brook trout (though it really is a char, *Salvelinus fontinalis*). When Europeans crossed the continental divide to the Pacific watershed, they found large fish – similar in appearance to European salmon – that were silvery when they left the sea and which swam up the rivers to spawn. Understandably enough, these fish were also called 'salmon', though they are not closely related to the Atlantic salmon. Compared with the sleek, perfectly shaped Atlantic salmon, some Pacific salmon seem quite grotesque.

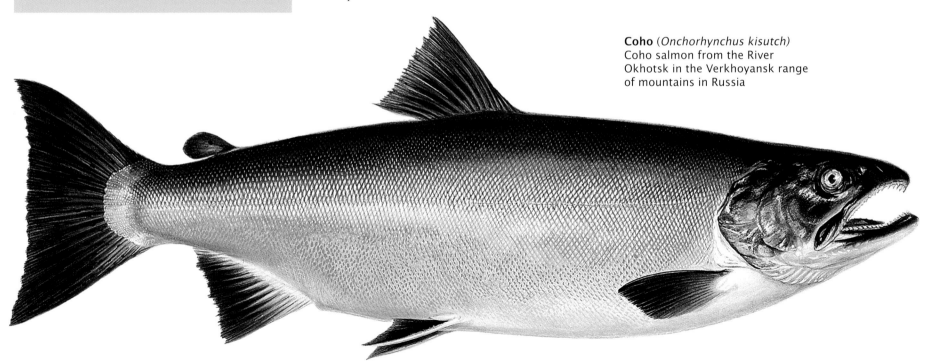

Coho (*Onchorhynchus kisutch*)
Coho salmon from the River Okhotsk in the Verkhoyansk range of mountains in Russia

Distribution of the Atlantic Salmon

General

The southern limit for breeding salmon occurs where water temperature in the rivers does not rise as high as the lethal temperature for adult salmon and their parr. Over the long term, this is in the range 21-23°C. Salmon can withstand temperatures up to 25°C for short periods. In the southernmost rivers of the Atlantic salmon's breeding range (such as the Loire-Allier, page 14), returning adult salmon and descending smolts time their respective runs to avoid the lethal summer temperatures (often around 30°C) attained in the lower reaches of these rivers.

Bearing in mind that hatching takes place in 115 days at 2.5°C, the northern limit for breeding salmon is where the river is not too cold for eggs to develop in time for the spring melt, and where the feeding season before the winter is long enough for fry to accumulate food reserves that will keep them going until the following spring.

On the eastern side of the Atlantic, the southernmost limit is 38°N (River Tagus, Portugal) and the northernmost 71°N (River Tana, Norway and smaller rivers in Varangerhalvøya), 4° 30' north of the Arctic Circle. On the North American side of the Atlantic, the southernmost limit is at about 41°N (rivers draining into Long Island Sound) and the northernmost limits, 60°N in rivers draining to Ungava Bay, 6° 30' south of the Arctic Circle, and 64°N (Kapisigdlit River, Greenland), 2° 30' south of the Arctic Circle. This 11° difference in latitude between the most northerly salmon breeding rivers of Canada and northern Europe is a consequence of the relatively warm North Atlantic Current (the continuation of the Gulf Stream) washing the shores of northern Europe, and the icy Labrador Current bringing chill to the Canadian coast. Southern Greenland is bathed by the Irminger Current, which is warmer than the Labrador Current.

Salmon Breeding Distribution in North America

Salmon occur naturally from the Koksoak River of Ungava Bay and the Kapisigdlit (the only Salmon river in Greenland) south to the Housatonic and Connecticut Rivers. Many North American rivers lost their spawning runs mainly through damming and pollution. Anthony Netboy (1974) described, for instance, how a dam 27 feet (8.1 metres) high was built at Lawrence on the Merrimack River in 1847; *"By 1860, the last salmon that spawned above the dam had lived its span of life, and none has ever been seen since."* He also refers to Maine, which had 20 thriving salmon rivers before the white man raped the countryside, the logging industry *"jammed the rivers for miles, and dumped mountains of sawdust into the river beds."*

In recent years, there have been considerable efforts made in both the USA and Canada to try and re-establish salmon in rivers from which they had been exterminated. As Jack T.H. Fenety stated, in the 3rd International Salmon Symposium at Biarritz in October 1986, *"There is an almost unbelievable concentrated construction programme of expensive fishways and other remedial measures in the hoped for return of Atlantic salmon to rivers where salmon have not been seen since George Washington was President!"*

Migratory routes (marked yellow) of salmon through the Atlantic to North American rivers

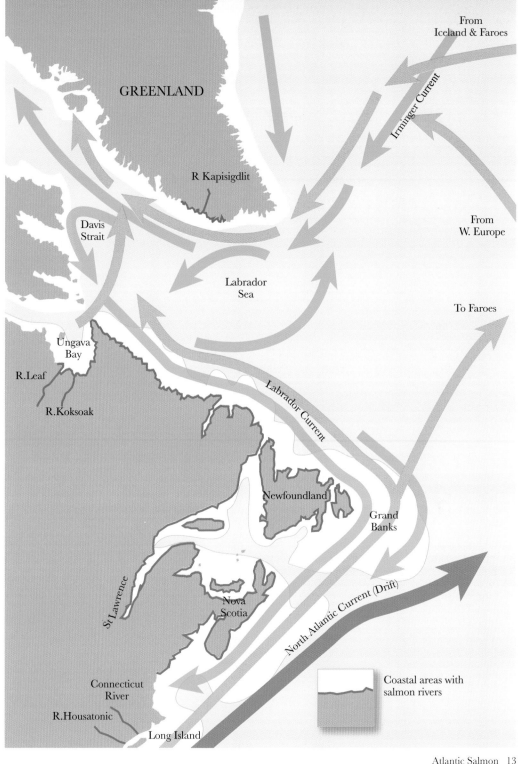

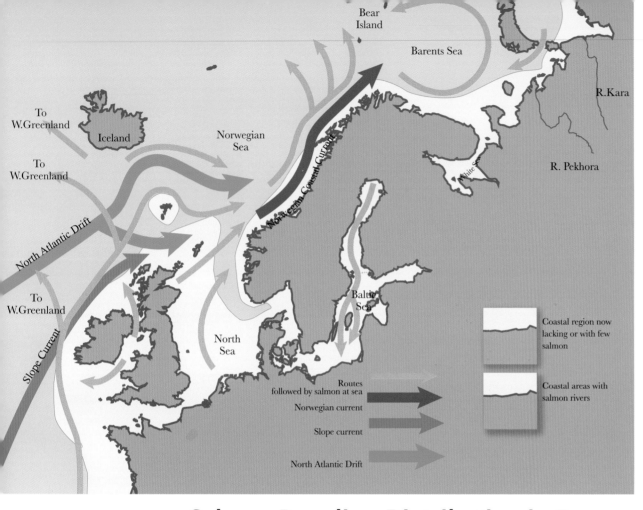

Salmon Breeding Distribution in Europe

Migratory routes of
salmon through the Atlantic
to European rivers

In Europe, the Atlantic salmon naturally occurs in nearly all clean rivers from the Tagus (Portugal) northwards up to and including Iceland and Norway's North Cape, and eastwards to the Pechora and Kara Rivers in Siberian Russia. Exceptions are a few glacier-fed rivers that carry huge quantities of suspended solids, and those with impassable falls close to the tide.

Very many European rivers have completely lost their stocks of salmon as a consequence of gross pollution (usually in the lower reaches), or through damming. Thus, the Portuguese rivers Tagus, Douro, Mondego and Lima now have very few salmon, or lack them entirely. The Elbe and Oder in Germany, and most of the Baltic rivers of Finland and the Baltic States are also devoid of salmon or have only small runs.

As in North America, great strides have been made in recent years to re-establish runs of salmon in rivers that have lost them, such as the Rhine and Thames. That most polluted of rivers, the Mersey (which flows past Liverpool) had no run at all throughout the 20th century. Then in 2001 three salmon tried to run the river. In 2002 there were 26. If fish-passes where built on the weirs above the tide, salmon might once more swim through the heart of the City of Manchester to spawn in the Mersey's clean headwaters.

In some of the greatest rivers, salmon have to run long distances from the sea to the spawning grounds. The best example is the Loire-Allier where, since about 1980, many fish-passes have been built to permit fish to reach the headwaters. From the mouth of the Loire, salmon swim about 330 miles (530 kilometres) to the confluence with the Allier. Because the lower Loire experiences high water temperatures in summer (often lethally exceeding 30°C) salmon make their upstream journey between autumn and spring, and lie up in the cooler headwater pools before spawning the following autumn. Most then enter the Allier and continue for a further 225 miles (360 kilometres) into the Massif Central, upstream of Langeac.

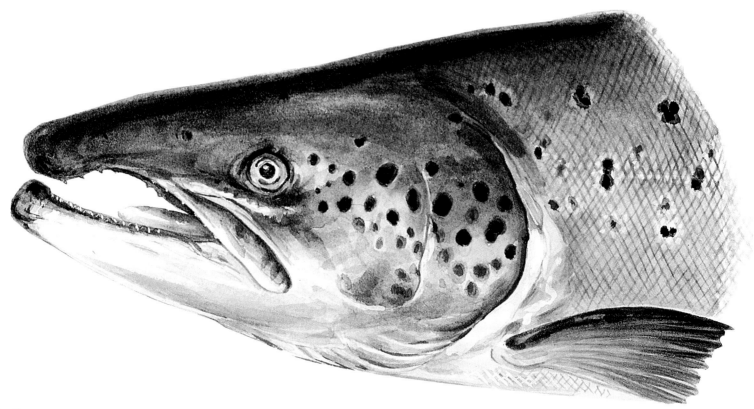

Land-Locked Salmon

Over 50 rivers flowing into the vastness of Lake Ontario (7,500 square miles or 19,500 square kilometres) once produced salmon smolts that grew to large salmon in the fresh water of the lake. These smolts never moved downstream through the St. Lawrence to feed and grow in the Atlantic. The immense population of Lake Ontario Atlantic salmon became extinct because of over-fishing, logging, damming and pollution. The last one was recorded from Wilmot Creek in 1896. The Ontario system was later stocked with Pacific salmon and they now thrive there.

Sweden's Lake Vanern and Russia's Lake Lagoda have populations of Blanklax that spawn in the inflowing streams and which grow to several pounds/kilograms in the lake.

There are many populations of very small land-locked salmon. Ouananiche occur in Lake St. John (Quebec) and Sebago in the lakes of New England, New Brunswick and Nova Scotia. In Norway, Smablank, rarely attaining half-a-pound in weight (about 500g), occur above an impassable waterfall on the upper Namsen, while Blege can be found in Lake Byglandsfjord.

Head of a male
land-locked salmon

Distribution of the Salmon at Sea

The maps on pages 13 and 14 also show the routes taken by salmon to and between their Atlantic feeding grounds, and the major oceanic currents.

Salmon from the rivers of northern Spain, France and the western parts of the British Isles head north-east with the Slope Current that follows the edge of the Continental Shelf. Fish from rivers flowing into the North Sea head north to pick up the Norwegian Coastal Current. These salmon are thus drawn to major feeding areas around the Faroe Islands and the Norwegian Sea. Those juvenile salmon leaving the rivers of northern Russia head west and then make an anti-clockwise migration around the Barents Sea, reaching as far north as Bear Island. Baltic salmon remain in the Baltic.

Some European salmon appear to swim across the North Atlantic straight away, eventually picking up the Irminger Current, and heading to the Davis Strait and coastal waters off West Greenland. After a first winter feeding around the Faroes and Norwegian Sea, some European salmon travel west to feed off Greenland.

Salmon from North American rivers move north to the Grand Banks and then move against the Labrador Current to feed in the Labrador Sea, Davis Strait and the coastal waters off Greenland. Some also head eastwards to feed around the Faroe Islands and in the Norwegian Sea.

It appears that whilst salmon from North America and Europe mix on their feeding grounds, there is no evidence of salmon from either continent getting lost and spawning on the other continent (i.e., the one on which they were not born).

Marine feeding grounds of juvenile salmon are areas with a fairly restricted range of sea surface temperatures. Having left their natal rivers, smolts seek a sea surface temperature of 8-10°C and later feed in a range of 4-10°C. (See also pages 56-61)

Looking out over the ocean's vastness from a ship or a headland, there appears to be a constancy of salty water. One could be forgiven for imagining that sea is sea; all of it the same. That impression is completely wrong. As far as salmon are concerned, only a small area of the ocean provides suitable feeding grounds and, as I write this in 2004, the Atlantic salmon's feeding grounds are much smaller than they were in 1964. This, by the way, is nothing to do with the environmental hot-potato of 'global warming'. J.W.Hurrell has calculated the NAO Index back to 1880 and shown how it has oscillated, and with it the observed populations of adult salmon. The problem is this: the NAO Index has never been so high and salmon stocks so low for so long a period since records began. (See page 18)

A group of large salmon move under the Arctic ice

NAO High

NAO Low

'The North Atlantic Oscillation (NAO)…acts as a dominant control on the environment of the Atlantic salmon.'

R.R. Dickson and W.R. Turrell, in D. Mills (ed), *The Ocean Life of the Atlantic Salmon*, 2000

The North Atlantic Oscillation and Oceanic Distribution of Salmon

In the 1960s and early 1970s, the numbers of salmon returning to their spawning rivers from the North Atlantic were relatively large. Since then, especially in the 1980s and 1990s, the numbers returning have been very low, especially of multi-sea winter fish (see page 132). According to a long-term study of the North Esk River by a team led by W.M. Shearer, the number of smolts heading out to sea from that river had not declined over this period. Those findings indicate that mortality at sea has greatly increased. The Atlantic is sending back fewer adult salmon.

The North Atlantic Oscillation (NAO) is based on a differential in the atmospheric pressure that occurs in winter between the Icelandic Low and the Azores High. When this difference is great, the NAO Index is said to be high, and when the difference is small, the NAO Index is said to be low. Through the 1960s and early 1970s, the NAO Index was consistently low, whereas since the 1980s, the NAO Index has been consistently high.

How does this affect salmon?

In the long period of high NAO Index years that has been experienced since 1980 coastal water temperatures around western Europe have been higher than usual, while waters further north – especially off Greenland and in the north Norwegian Sea – have been much cooler than they were during the 1960s when the NAO Index was lower. Since the 1980s, there have been significantly more winter storms, greater wave heights and increased wave-driven currents. Increased rainfall in northern Europe (reduced in southern and central Europe) and increased movement of icebergs from the Greenland glaciers and polar ice-cap have reduced salinity, shifting and reducing in width the Norwegian Coastal Current, and possibly other major currents.

The consequence of the switch from the low NAO Index that prevailed in the bountiful 1960s and early 1970s to the high NAO Index since the 1980s has been a reduction in the oceanic feeding ground of the Atlantic salmon. Warming has pushed the southernmost feeding limit northwards, while cooling around Greenland and in the Barents and Norwegian Seas has pushed the northerly limit southwards. Those salmon that remain out at sea for two or more years are most affected, for they feed further north in the feeding grounds than do grilse (fish that return after only one year).

However, even as the juvenile salmon make their initial movements from their natal river estuaries and head northwards, a narrowing and speeding up of at least some currents have reduced these vitally important initial feeding areas. As noted on page 56, juvenile salmon that grow quickly are more likely to escape predation than those that grow slowly. It is not only to do with food availability. For juvenile salmon that move very close to the surface of the water, swimming in rougher seas requires far more effort and therefore more food

Three salmon in the River Findhorn, Scotland

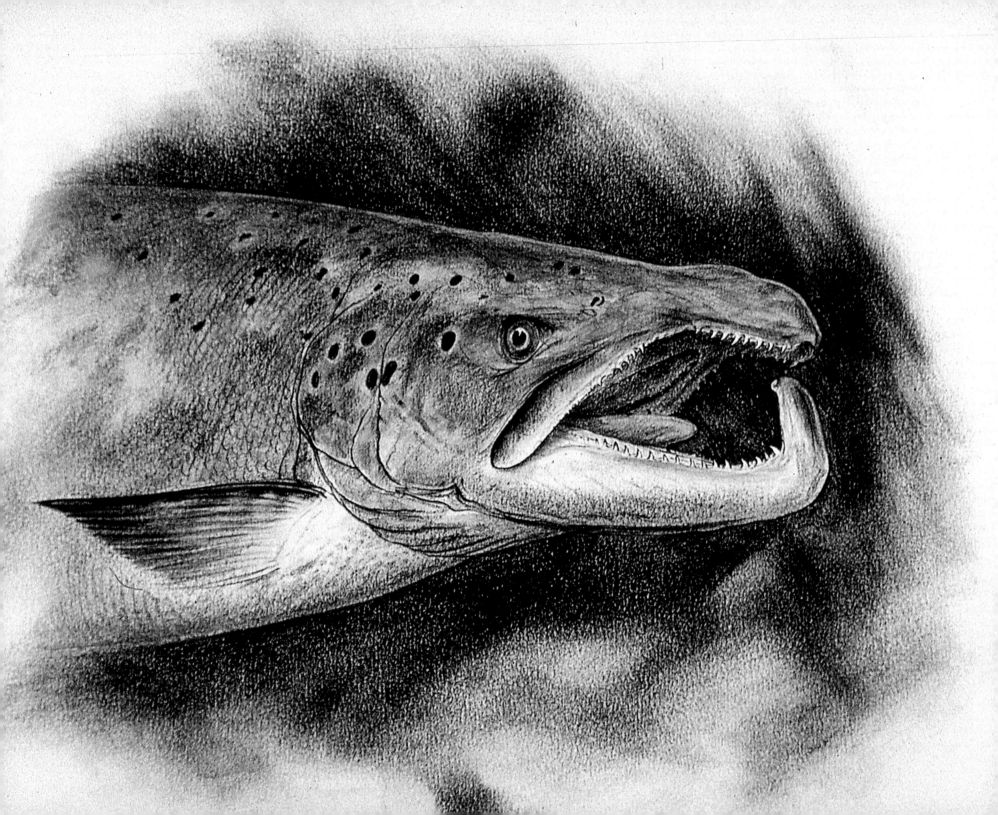

CHAPTER TWO

LIFE IN THE NURSERY

'By spawning time considerable changes have taken place in the appearance of the salmon. They are no longer the magnificent silvery fish that entered the river…'

J.W. Jones, *The Salmon*, 1959

Head of a mature cock salmon, showing its grotesque kype (hooked lower jaw) elongated snout and large teeth. Salmon have been observed moving rocks on the redds with their kypes

As spawning time approaches – autumn or very early winter in most rivers, though in some late-run streams salmon may spawn as late as January or February – the hen's colouration becomes first a matt-pewter and then a drab dark brown-grey. The cock fish, in contrast, begins to gain some brighter colours. First, small areas of red-brown mottling appear on the gill covers and this autumnal 'tartan', echoing the oranges, reds and browns of the falling leaves, spreads onto the flanks of the fish. Associated with these colour changes is a wasting away of the scales. It has been postulated that the scale tissue is absorbed by the body to nurture changes that take place in the body structure before spawning.

The most fascinating change in the cock salmon is the growth of the grotesque hooked jaw, or kype. The front of the lower jaw extends and then curves upwards to form a hook. The upper jaw also extends, usually with a slight downward curve, and the tip of the hooked kype fits into a notch at the end of the upper jaw. This is a skeletal change, requiring lots of calcium salts as well as fat and protein. Because the salmon does not feed as the kype develops, the materials needed must be taken from stores laid down at sea (fat and protein), or from other structures (calcium perhaps from scales or from other parts of the skeleton).

Though the kype gives the head of the cock salmon a somewhat aggressive appearance, there are few recorded instances of it being used as a weapon against competing cock fish. Prior to mating, a cock will chase interlopers around his pool and may actually ram those slow to move on, but, as in most sexual displays amongst competing males, there is usually more bluster and bluff than serious violence.

Before successful mating can occur, the eggs must form in the ovaries of the female fish and milt (a creamy fluid containing sperm) must form in the testes of the males. In spring-run salmon, ovaries and testes are undeveloped when the fish arrive back in the river, so that most of the body materials needed for maturation come from muscle tissue and stored reserves. In autumn-run salmon, much of the egg and milt development occurs before the fish return to the river, so these developments can utilize digested food. Thus, whilst the average hen salmon produces about 750 eggs per pound (500 grams) of her body weight, hens that run in spring produce 20-40% fewer eggs than autumn-run hens of the same size. Furthermore, the eggs of spring-run salmon are slightly smaller than those of autumn-run fish.

Eventually, a female salmon pairs with the male of her choice. His role is to ensure that her eggs are fertilized, even though he may not fertilize them all himself.

The henfish digging the redds

The henfish covering the redds

A spawning pair of salmon

Legal Protection

For many hundreds of years the Atlantic salmon has been rigorously protected by law in most of its native countries.

"No young salmon may be taken or destroyed by nets, at mill dams or in other places, from the middle of April till the Nativity of St John the Baptist [26 June] from the waters of the Lone [Lune], Wyre, Mersee [Mersey], Rybble [Ribble] and all other waters in the County of Lancaster."

"No salmon can be taken from Michaelmas Day [29 September] to the Purification of Our Lady [2 February] because that salmons be not seasonable in the said waters in time aforesaid."

Richard II of England,
Duchy Court Rolls, 1389-90

The first of these restrictions prevented the catching of salmon smolts heading downstream to the sea, whereas the second prevented the capture of adult salmon before spawning (this occurs in early December on the rivers mentioned) and allowed the surviving kelts time to get back to sea after spawning.

Spawning fish on the redds. A henfish will often be attended by two or three cockfish – whilst displaying ritual combat between themselves, one cock will mate, others may follow

Egg-laying

The hen salmon will choose a suitable area of gravel (the redd) in which she will lay all her eggs. Her choice is based partly on the size of the gravel (up to about golf-ball size); the depth of water (in most rivers 6-12 inches, or 15-30 centimetres); and the rate of the flow (ideally 12-18 inches/second, or 30-45 centimetres/second). The eggs need to be protected by a layer of pebbles that are massive enough to resist being washed away by spates, and sufficiently loosely-packed to allow a good through-flow of well-oxygenated water. Some redds may be in water so shallow that the salmons' backs are out of the water during mating. Redds are often sited close to deeper water, where the fish may rest before and after mating, and where sanctuary can be sought from predators.

As spawning time approaches, the hen salmon, often accompanied by the cock, swims to and fro across the gravel looking for a suitable location for her nest. Once this has been found, the hen turns onto her side and flaps the flat of her tail violently against the gravel bottom. This action disturbs some of the gravel, which washes away downstream with the current and a shallow depression is formed in the gravel river bed. If she rests, the cock fish may sidle up next to her and start 'quivering'. This quivering action by the male either encourages the hen to continue cutting her nest, or initiates actual spawning when the nest is deep enough (as measured by the hen, using her anal fin). During this quivering, the male's mouth opens, his gill covers flare and his fins become erect, while muscular spasms pass down his body.

When the hen salmon is satisfied that the nest is deep enough, she settles her body right down into the depression she has made. The male swims alongside her, quivering, and orgasm is achieved. During their climax, both sexes have mouths and gills agape. The female sheds a stream of eggs into her nest which are fertilized by the cloud of milt simultaneously produced by the male.

After spawning, the cock swims away while the female moves a short distance upstream of the nest. Once again she turns onto her side and flaps her tail violently against the gravel bottom. This time, the gravel she disturbs is washed downstream to settle over the eggs that she has just laid in the nest. If she still has eggs to shed, this will also create another depression in the gravel for another nest, and the mating process can be repeated.

Salmon eggs are sticky, so that they adhere to each other and to the gravel in the bottom of the nest. Relatively few are therefore lost and washed away. In very heavily stocked streams, however, late arriving hens often cut their nests into those of hens that have already spawned. Then the eggs from the earlier nest may be lost as they are disturbed by the later nest builder and washed downstream. In well-managed rivers that have rather more spawning fish than the available redds can accommodate, the excess are harvested (see p124).

An opportunistic brown trout feeds off the eggs scattered by a spawning salmon

A cock fish coaxes a hen onto the redds, typical activity of pre-spawning fish

The Role of Precocious Parr

W.M. Shearer found that 64% of smolts heading to sea from the North Esk River were female, 36% male. The sex ratio of salmon returning to spawn is usually 60-70% female, 30-40% male. Adult females thus greatly outnumber adult males and this would seem to indicate a potential major problem of there not being enough males to service all the females. In practice, the problem does not arise for two reasons.

Promiscuous males

Cock salmon are highly promiscuous and will mate with more than one female. Indeed, even when they have exhausted their supply of milt, 'spent' cock salmon will continue to court and mate with females, even though they are unable to fertilize the eggs. Even so, these eggs may still become fertilized.

Precocious parr

The eggs of female salmon may be fertilized by milt from precocious male parr that become sexually mature without going to sea. These little chaps may nip in and shed their milt while a pair of adult fish is copulating. Thanks to these sexually precocious male parr, the female's eggs may be fertilized, even if the adult male involved has no more milt of his own to achieve the task.

Studies have shown that an average of 12% of all eggs are fertilized by parr (in one study up to 25.2%), and not by adult male salmon, and that up to 70% of all male parr may be sexually mature.

Whilst observations indicate that the presence of a quivering (though spent) adult male is important in stimulating the hen fish to spawn, a study in Newfoundland, by J. Hutchings and R.A. Myers, found male parr capable of mating with hen salmon in the absence of adult males. It is possible that the salmon's behavioural pattern may evolve and follow that of the seatrout, where the female fish go to sea and grow large but a high proportion of the males remain in the river as much smaller brown trout.

The rigours of precocious sexual activity result in a higher mortality among male parr compared with their female counterparts, and consequently in a lower proportion of males among smolts going out to sea. This, in turn, results in a lower ratio of adult males to female fish returning from the sea.

Some females fail to mate and are sometimes caught by anglers early the following season. The large egg-mass can be felt in the body cavity and the abdomen appears bloated. These unspawned hens are known as baggots.

Precocious female parr have been recorded from land-locked populations of Atlantic salmon (page 25), but only very rarely in sea-going river populations. One specimen, from the River Elorn (France), weighed 6 ounces (150 grams), was 9 inches (22 centimetres) in length, and produced 256 ova.

The Kellah Burn on the Tyne system: the mid-winter stream seems lifeless, yet in the gravel redds, salmon eggs are developing slowly

Hatching

The first sign of development is the appearance of two black spots in the egg. These are the eyes of the developing fish and when they appear the eggs are known as eyed-ova. The eggs hatch in 70-160 days depending on water temperature. In the warmer climates found in the south of the salmon's range (Spain, France, Ireland and southern Britain), all are hatched by March-April. In the cooler north of the range (Russia, Fenno-Scandia, Iceland and Canada), hatching occurs between late May and early July. Up in the Arctic, the salmon rivers of Lapland and Kola are often ice-bound as late as June. It is vital that fry emergence in these rivers coincides with the end of the ice melt and the beginning of the short summer.

Ovum

Eyed ovum

Close to the hatch

Hatching

From egg to fry: the stages of the young salmon's development

Yolk-sack

Alevin, yolk sack almost absorbed

Fry

Fingerling

Parr

Early Development

The Alevin

The egg eventually hatches into an alevin, a pale orange or pinkish creature less than one inch (about 2 centimetres) in length. At this stage, the alevin is recognisably fish-shaped, but it has a large yolk sac attached underneath to provide it with nourishment. Alevins are highly vulnerable to predators, for they cannot swim quickly to avoid them. It is essential that alevins remain in the sanctuary of the redd until they have absorbed the cumbersome yolk sac, can swim reasonably well. and are ready to feed actively. To this end, the tiny creatures demonstrate the automatic responses of negative photokinesis, positive geotaxis and positive rheotaxis: they move down into the gravel away from light and towards gravity, and they lie with their heads pointing into the flow of oxygenated water passing through the gravel.

The Fry

By the time the yolk sacs are exhausted, the alevins have developed camouflaged colouration and become fry. Their automatic responses to external stimuli change. They now exhibit positive photokinesis and negative geotaxis, and move up through the gravel towards the light and against the pull of gravity. This would be dangerous if carried through unchecked so that the fry moved straight up into the water where they could either be swept away by the current or easily noticed by predators. To avoid this, the young fry automatically exhibit a counteracting positive thigmotaxis; a tactile response which ensures that they keep their undersides in contact with the gravel. Continuing positive rheotaxis makes the fry maintain their position facing into the current. It also helps them start feeding for, as water passes into their open mouths and out via the gills, it carries with it microscopic food particles (diatoms, minute larvae, etc.). This passively-gathered food is digested in the gut and eventually triggers the active feeding response.

The fry disperse through the nursery stream. One study showed that the fry from one particular redd had dispersed as far as 185 yards (166 metres) upstream and 825 yards (743 metres) downstream of the redd four weeks after emerging from the gravel nest. Dispersal occurs mainly at night, presumably to avoid predators.

As the fry grows, between eight and eleven regularly spaced, dark, oval-shaped marks (parr-marks) start to appear along its flanks. Once these distinctive marks have developed, the fry has become a parr.

Some salmon hatcheries experience problems in getting very young fry to start feeding. High mortality rates can occur where there is insufficient flow to introduce those first few food particles into the young fishes' mouths in order to stimulate active feeding. Fry that have not yet started feeding are referred to as unfed fry, while those that have become active feeders are called fed fry.

What Exactly is a Parr?

It is difficult to appreciate today, early in the 21st century, how little was known about the natural world even 150 years ago. It was not until late in the eighteenth century that the Swedish naturalist Carl Linné (or Linnaeus) established the modern system of scientific names and classification of plants and animals. This system is the foundation upon which scientific natural history is based. It encouraged the study of relationships between species, and the determination of what were distinct species and what were not.

Here is just one example of how our knowledge has progressed. Even as recently as the end of the 18th century, many people considered that the drake mallard and the drabber female mallard (then simply called the 'wild duck') were separate species. Incredibly, even the great Linnaeus agreed with them and named the drake *Anas platyrhynchos* and the duck *Anas boscas*. To the modern naturalist, this is incomprehensible. How could the relationship between male and female in such a common species as the mallard not have been observed and understood by that time?

In 1836, William Yarrell (*A History of British Fishes*, Vol 2) attempted the first thorough review of British fish and included, 'The Parr, or Samlet'. He gave it the scientific name *Salmo salmulus*, and insisted, "*That the Parr is not the young of the salmon, or indeed of any other of the larger species of Salmonidae, as still considered by some, is sufficiently obvious.*"

Yarrell gave two main pieces of evidence that the parr was a species in its own right, and not a juvenile salmon. First, he stated: "*by summer the 'fry' of salmon have all gone to sea, so the parr remaining in the river cannot be salmon fry*". This, of course, displayed a complete ignorance of the life-cycle of the salmon. Secondly, Yarrell pointed out: "*parr are common in many rivers where most adult salmon are removed with nets and spears.*" In those days it was not realised how few spawning salmon are needed to restock a clean river (see pages 105ff).

Some others accepted that salmon parr were juvenile salmon, but believed that there was also a distinct species called 'parr', *Salmo salmulus*. For instance, a certain Mr Rooper stated that "*The transverse bars on Salmo salmulus are more numerous, more strongly marked, longer and narrower than in the parr of the salmon; the colour of the eye is totally different, though I cannot describe the difference…*"

In the year that Yarrell's tome reached the bookshops, John Shaw of Drumlanrig, in the Nith valley (Dumfriesshire) was completing a four-year study of the freshwater stages of the salmon life-cycle. He raised eggs through the alevin and fry stages to parr, and then on to smolt. He then observed the smolts swimming downstream towards the sea.

In 1893, the eminent naturalist, Frank Buckland, firmly established the parr's place in the salmon's life cycle (*Familiar History of British Fishes*), stating: "*I, for my part, say that such a fish does not exist as a distinct species*". The 'young of salmon' were thus listed in the Salmon Fisheries Acts of 1861 and 1865 for England and Wales by the names of fry, samlet, smolt, smelt, skirling or scarling, parr, spawn, pink, lastspring, hepper, lastbrood, gravelling, shed, scad, blue-fin, black-tip, fingerling, brandling, broadling… and several others.

'…I have discovered what is meant by a parr; they are what we call gravelin, and we suppose them to be produced from some part of the pea of the salmon which has been imperfect, or been carried away without due impregnation.'

O'Gorman, *The Practice of Angling*, Vol 2, 1845.

The activity of spawning continues into the night – in many ways a safer time for the fish. This night study was based on the River South Tyne

The Territory of the Parr

A salmon parr is a territorial creature and does not usually tolerate other parr within close visual distance. The riverbed, therefore, becomes divided into a number of 'territories'. Parr that cannot obtain their own territories are forced to move away. As parr grow, they enlarge their territories, ousting their weaker neighbours. Mortality is especially high in the first few months of life. One study indicated an initial mortality of about one percent per day in very well-stocked nursery streams. In less well-stocked streams, mortality is much lower as there is more free space into which displaced fish can move.

Parr density in well-stocked streams appears to depend upon three main factors. The first is water depth. Fry and parr in their first year (0+ parr) occur in higher densities in shallower water, whereas parr in their second and subsequent years (1+ parr) favour deeper water. It may be that 1+ parr choose the deeper water lies and force the 0+ parr to occupy shallower areas. Alternatively, 0+ parr may actually prefer very shallow water because aquatic predators (such as brown trout and chub) are less likely to hunt in shallows.

The structure of the streambed is also an important factor in territorialism. Parr densities are much lower where the bed is flat fine gravel or sand than where it contains lots of cobbles and boulders. In a nursery area in the River Lune, for example, parr were spaced an average of 16' 8" (5.2 metres) apart in an area of fairly flat gravel, and 3' 8" (1.1 metre) apart in an area of boulders and bedrock outcrops. It would seem that parr prefer lies with a 'home-stone' that acts as a focal point to which they can relate. It is also possible that large boulders acting as visual barriers prevent parr from seeing their close neighbours, thus allowing them to live in closer proximity to one another than they would in areas of featureless gravel. The addition of large boulders to a formerly flat streambed has often resulted in an increased density of parr.

The third factor in determining the carrying capacity of a nursery stream is the abundance of food. A study conducted in the Icelandic River Lax i Kjos found that parr densities were very high in the River Bugda (a tributary leading from the productive lake Meddelfelsvatn), where much food drifted downstream from the lake. By contrast, parr densities were very low further downstream, below the confluence with a cold, unproductive tributary.

In winter, when the water temperature has fallen below 7-10°C , parr seek deeper, slower water. They may go into hiding, and feeding is reduced. There are exceptions. In the rivers of northern Russia, Norway and Canada, where water temperatures exceed 10°C for only a short period, parr continue to feed and grow throughout the period that the river is not actually iced-up.

Parr are territorial creatures who keep their own ground in the rocks and hollows of the river bed

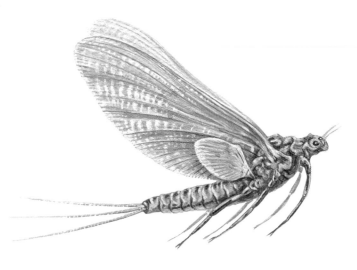

Mayfly leaving the water, newly hatched: good food for the salmon parr

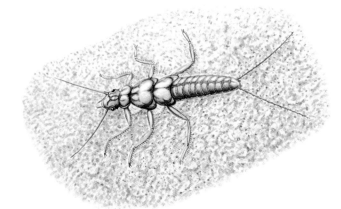

Stonefly nymphs are another popular source of nutrition for the parr

Food and Feeding

The feeding-lies of parr are usually close to distinct, though often very narrow, bands of current. These currents may be shared by several parr provided that they can feed without interfering with each another. Current flow is far more complex over a stretch of river with boulders, cobbles and bedrock outcrops than over a flat, featureless riverbed. We have seen (page 41) that bouldered stretches hold a higher density of parr than areas of flat bed. It is possible that the more complex flow patterns associated with these stretches and the way they distribute the food brought downstream could be a factor. Studies have also shown that larger parr tend to choose faster currents, which deliver food items to the waiting fish at a quicker rate than do slower flows.

A study from the River Tilt found that about three-quarters of all food taken by salmon parr consisted of items brought downstream with the current. The other quarter comprised immature nymphs and larvae (Ephemeroptera, Plecoptera, Trichoptera and *Simulium*) that the parr had actually grubbed up from the riverbed close to their feeding lies.

Of food items taken that were drifting downstream, the proportions taken from on the surface (adult winged insects, mostly of the aforementioned groups standing on the surface), and from slightly below the surface (mainly nymphs and pupae rising to hatch at the surface) were roughly equal and greatly exceeded drifting food items taken close to the river bed.

This indicates that parr concentrate their feeding attention at or very close to the surface, rather than through the entire water depth, particularly when aquatic insects are rising to hatch at the water surface, and hatched flies are standing on the surface itself. About one-third of drifting foods were taken as soon as they entered the feeding lie, but two-thirds were taken slightly downstream of the lie, after the parr had inspected the items closely.

Observations on rivers in north-west England suggest that parr are opportunistic feeders, taking various food items as and when they occur. On one occasion, during a sparse summer evening hatch of blue-winged olives (*Seratella ignita*), the parr ignored bottom-foods completely and concentrated on taking both the nymphs rising to hatch and the winged sub-imagos (that anglers refer to as 'duns') from the surface itself. Close to sunset, however, the parr turned their attentions to huge numbers of dead and dying female imagos (spinners) of the autumn dun (*Ecdyonurus dispar*), that had laid their eggs and had collapsed, exhausted, onto the surface of the river. During one afternoon and evening in late May, the parr on a particular stretch of river were observed to change diet six times as successive hatches of different aquatic fly species occurred.

Several studies have indicated that salmon parr take a far smaller proportion of land-bred (terrestrial) insects than do trout parr. This could be because trout parr tend to choose lies close to the river bank, near overhanging marginal vegetation, whereas salmon parr take up lies right across the river and may even avoid the river margins. This marginal vegetation generates most of the land-bred insects that reach the river surface and so will tend to benefit the trout parr most. In rivers with large populations of both salmon and trout, such a separation of feeding-lies helps to reduce competition between the two closely-related species.

Small pool: typical habitat of salmon parr. The adult salmon are unable to pass this waterfall

A parr will become a smolt as it begins its migration to sea, losing the parr-marks on reaching the salt water. Smolts come together as a shoal on reaching the sea. Initially, smolts display spots only on the operculum

The Smolt

Although parr have distinct feeding-lies that they occupy from spring to autumn, they do move around within the river system. When the river is in flood, they must take shelter well away from the heavy flow. When the flood subsides, they return to their lies. In autumn, when food production in the river slows down, they move into deeper water, up or downstream of their summer lies. A parr that has attained a length of about 4 inches (10 centimetres) in autumn will usually become a smolt and head to sea in the following spring. In autumn, when the parr move into deeper water, most of those that will become smolts in spring move downstream from their feeding-lies. This is the first movement the young salmon make towards the sea.

As day length increases in late winter and spring, the appearance of the juvenile salmon changes dramatically as it prepares for life at sea. The body becomes more streamlined and the snout more pointed. The tail becomes more slender and the tail fin more markedly forked. A layer of guanin is laid down beneath the outer layer of the skin, which hides the parr-marks and the camouflaged colouration that protected the fish in the river. It now takes on a silvery appearance, like so many marine fish, with blackish tail and pectoral fins.

The smolt run in any river may last between four and six weeks. In many rivers, they begin their journey to the sea once the water temperature exceeds 10°C. In cooler, more northerly rivers (especially in northern Canada, Iceland, Fenno-Scandia and Russia), migration is triggered by temperature rises from the winter minimum of close to freezing. While they were parr the juvenile salmon were territorial and actively eschewed each other's company, but now there is a benefit in coming together. For their seaward migration, the smolts find safety in numbers by banding together in loose shoals.

Most of the downstream journey is achieved by passively dropping back with the current, tail first and facing upstream. In slow pools, or where they pass through a lake, the smolts head downstream and actively swim in that direction. Movement occurs mainly at night, but by late spring migration continues well into daylight and sometimes throughout the day.

There have been few observations of the speed at which smolts pass downstream, and most of these are from fairly short rivers. They give a downstream progress of up to about 3.2 miles (5 kilometres) per day. In much longer rivers, however, progress needs to be significantly faster. In the long Loire-Allier system, smolts have been observed to move downstream at rates averaging about 12.5 miles (20 kilometres) per day, though 44 miles (70 kilometres) in a day has been recorded. Loire-Allier smolts may take about 45 days to reach their estuary. By comparison, on the fairly short (30-mile, 50-kilometre) Ribble-Hodder, in north west England, it only takes about 10 days for smolts leaving the headwaters to reach their estuary and they do so travelling at much slower rates.

It is likely that the smolt population of each river system has an inbuilt timing that gauges the speed of downstream migration so that arrival in the estuary coincides with optimum inshore sea temperatures for the smolts to start their life in the ocean (page 56). Moreover, smolts in the longer and more southern rivers of the Atlantic salmon's range (such as the Loire) must also time their downstream migration to avoid lethally high summer temperatures in the lower reaches of the river.

Post-smolts, the term given to smolts on reaching the sea, take on the familiar silver pigmentation of the adult salmon

The Age of the Smolt

When it comes to the life cycle of the salmon, Mother Nature never puts all her eggs in one basket. The age at which parr become smolts is a case in point. If an entire year-class of parr (all the parr born in one year) from a particular river were all to go to sea as smolts in the same year, a catastrophe in the river mouth might wipe out the whole lot. Similarly, if all the parr remained in the river until their smaller, slower-growing brothers and sisters were ready to become smolts, they could all be wiped out by a catastrophe in the nursery headwaters.

Some parr grow more quickly than others and may become smolts after just over one year (1+ parr), whereas others may go to sea after just over two (2+ parr), three (3+ parr), four (4+ parr) or even more years of living in the river.

In general, parr grow more quickly and go to sea earlier in the rivers in the south of the salmon's range. In France's River Allier, for example, up to 95% of wild 1+ parr become smolts (at an average length of 6 inches or 15.5 centimetres) and almost all the rest become smolts at 2+ (at an average length of 8 inches or 18 centimetres). By contrast, in the rivers of northern England, only 1% of 1+ parr become smolts; 85% smolting at 2+ and up to 15% at 3+. On the Spey and the Aberdeenshire Dee in Scotland, 65% of smolts were 2+ parr, 30% 3+ parr and about 4% 4+ parr. In Iceland, most parr become smolts after 3-5 years of river life. In northern Norway, Finland and Russia, the smolt stage is reached after 3-7 years.

Parr in North American rivers take longer to reach smolt stage than in most of Europe. Overall, 5% of North American salmon parr become smolts after one year (cf. 20% in Europe); 40% after two years (cf. 55% in Europe); 35% after three years (cf. 15% in Europe) and about 20% at four years or older (cf. fewer than 5% in Europe). In rivers draining into Ungava Bay in north east Canada, it takes 4-8 years for parr to reach smolt stage, with an average of five years.

Post-smolts feed voraciously on reaching the sea, sometimes quite near to the surface

The Predators of Fry, Parr and Smolt

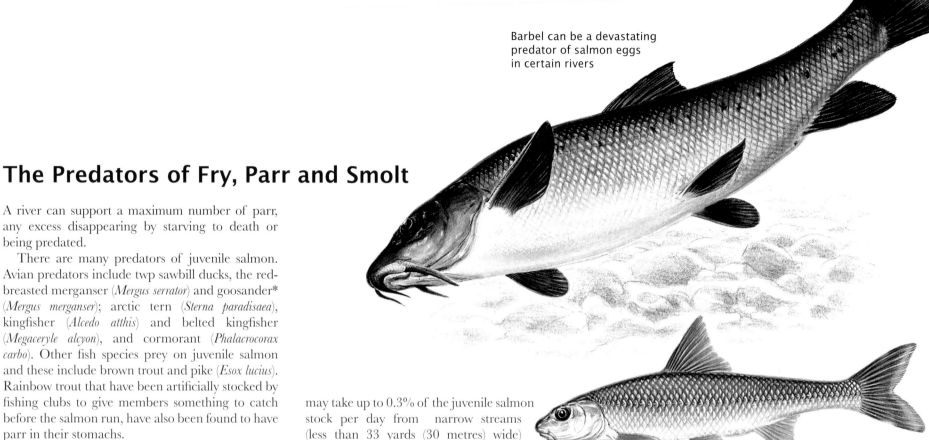

Barbel can be a devastating predator of salmon eggs in certain rivers

The gudgeon, another opportunistic consumer of salmon eggs

A river can support a maximum number of parr, any excess disappearing by starving to death or being predated.

There are many predators of juvenile salmon. Avian predators include two sawbill ducks, the red-breasted merganser (*Mergus serrator*) and goosander* (*Mergus merganser*); arctic tern (*Sterna paradisaea*), kingfisher (*Alcedo atthis*) and belted kingfisher (*Megaceryle alcyon*), and cormorant (*Phalacrocorax carbo*). Other fish species prey on juvenile salmon and these include brown trout and pike (*Esox lucius*). Rainbow trout that have been artificially stocked by fishing clubs to give members something to catch before the salmon run, have also been found to have parr in their stomachs.

Anglers and fishery managers often consider that the loss of a single parr to a predator is one too many. But is it? Are not the predators simply taking the weaker fish and excess numbers that would never survive anyway? Are they not cleaning up the river, and preventing massive losses through disease, caused by overcrowding?

The following are conclusions from some scientific studies:

Scotland in general

(Freshwater Fisheries Laboratory, 1990s) Each goosander and merganser takes 3-8 juvenile salmon per day from rivers in southern Scotland (where other prey species are abundant), but up to 61 per day from rivers in northern Scotland (where other prey species are scarce). On the River Dee, they may take up to 0.3% of the juvenile salmon stock per day from narrow streams (less than 33 yards (30 metres) wide) and up to 0.4% of the stock per day from wider streams.

North Esk River, Scotland

(W.M. Shearer et al., 1987) Control of goosanders and mergansers would result in an increase of 35% in the adult salmon run. In other words, these two predators take far more than the surplus of fry, parr and smolts. One goosander will devour 1,000 smolts and 4,550 parr in a 91-day breeding season.

River Bush, Ireland

(G.J.A. Kennedy & J.E. Greer, 1988) Cormorants take 2,500 smolts per day during the month-long run to sea. These smolts are not from the surplus fry and parr (i.e. those that were never going to survive); they are from the holding-capacity of the river.

* In North America the goosander is called the merganser.

A large pike (*Exox lucius*) will take salmon up to at least 10lb (5kg)

River Pollett, New Brunswick, Canada

(P.F. Elson, 1962) At a population density of two belted kingfishers per mile (1.6 kilometres), one-third of parr are predated. With four birds per mile, the salmon smolt production in the river is halved. Following kingfisher control measures, the river's smolt run increased from about 3,000 per annum to 13,600-24,000 per annum.

River Miramichi, New Brunswick, Canada

(H.C. White, 1957) Parr production would increase by 1.9 million if mergansers* were culled (they ate 37% of the river's stock of parr). White also calculated that, on the River Margaree (Nova Scotia), one merganser takes 150 pounds (68 kilograms) of salmon parr per breeding season.

River Restigouche, New Brunswick

(J.M. Anderson, 1986) A three-year cull of mergansers resulted in a smolt run increase of 170,000.

There is no doubt that avian predators can make serious inroads into a river's smolt run, and consequently affect the numbers of returning adult salmon.

The question of whether or not to control the numbers of predators to increase the runs of adult salmon is a political one. Were it a purely economic issue, predators would be controlled (not exterminated) so that more salmon might be harvested by rod and net. However, the bird protection lobby is large and vociferous on both sides of the Atlantic. Traditionally, politicians have paid more heed to the bird protectionists than to those fewer voters with interests vested in commercial salmon netting or sport fishing. This has been true even where improved salmon fishing might bring important economic benefits to otherwise disadvantaged riverside communities. Nevertheless, while natural predators do make significant inroads into salmon stocks, they do not threaten the continued existence of salmon in any river.

Brown trout, despite being closely related to the salmon, have no qualms about feeding on salmon eggs and alevins

A large chalkstream Brown trout from the River Test, England

Large Trout and Juvenile Salmon

Under experimental conditions, a model of a large brown trout was moved close to feeding parr. The parr immediately stopped feeding and, 20 minutes after the potential predator had been removed, their feeding rate was 67% lower than it had been before the model trout had appeared.

In a study conducted in Scotland's Shelligan Burn, a tributary of the River Almond, where salmon fry densities were high (about 500 per 120 square yards or 100 square metres), up to 90% of fry were predated by brown trout. In the main river, where fry densities were much lower (50 per 120 square yards) predation was almost nil. An experiment was then carried out in which a part of the river was enclosed, keeping out all predators. Intuitively, one would have expected the density of fry and parr within the enclosure eventually to become higher than in the unenclosed river, where predators could

feed. But this was not so. Losses of fry and parr were almost the same, suggesting that trout were selecting those fry and parr that were being displaced by more dominant parr and which would die anyway.

This is an example of density-dependent mortality and population regulation. When a prey population is high predation increases and the density is reduced. But when a prey population is low predation is reduced so that more potential prey survive to breed, and the population increases. However, this applies only in a wild population of both predator (trout) and prey (juvenile salmon). The situation will be very different where the predator is encouraged by human interference.

A Lesson from the River Test

The River Test is a chalkstream in Hampshire, in the South of England. It is, perhaps, the most famous trout river in the world. The Test was once also an excellent salmon river in its lower reaches, but today it is not. How good the Test once was as a salmon river can be gauged from Sidney Vines' *The English Chalkstreams* (1992). Below Romsey a "*few years ago when salmon were plentiful, fishing tickets were hard to come by – but these days have gone. No salmon were taken there in 1990...Broadlands produced 350 salmon a year...the score in 1990 was six...*" At Nursling, which used to produce an annual catch of around 500 salmon, only 95 were caught in 1990, "*which for these days is good.*"

Fishery owners and anglers have blamed netting at sea for the decline in Test salmon. In reality, they ought to look no further than upstream in the Test itself. Phenomenal numbers of huge brown and rainbow trout are stocked here every spring - and they are huge trout. Tony Hayter has listed the largest brown trout caught by the great dry-fly fisher F.M. Halford for the years 1879-1913. The average weight of Halford's annual record trout was 3 pounds 3 ounces (1.5 kilograms). His personal best ever was 4 pounds 9 ounces (2.2 kilograms) and he caught a total of 2,242 over these years, averaging 64 per annum. Today, even an angler of moderate ability would expect to catch far more trout from the Test if he fished as often as Halford did. Moreover, the average and maximum weights of modern Test trout would be far higher than in Halford's day.

What chance do small salmon parr and fry have in a river stuffed with large predatory fish that would love to eat them?

Following the dramatic decline of the salmon, one lower Test beat became a trout-fishing beat ...stocked heavily with big brown trout!

The height of folly is to stock a salmon river with Rainbow trout, for they eat the eggs, fry and parr of the salmon

CHAPTER THREE

AND OFF TO SEA
The mystery of it all

'For Salmon being fish of prey, and great feeders, Nature directs them to the Salt waters, as Physick to purge and cleanse them...And when they are fatted and glutted by all their long excessive Feeding in fresh Rivers, and have spawn'd in the latter end of the Year, repair to the Sea for warmness, and to be purged from the Gross Humours by the Calidity of the Saline Waters...'

Robert Howlett,
The Angler's Sure Guide, 1706

De-forested moorland with excessive land drainage and heavy animal stocking has ruined many upland salmon streams. There are now many policies in place to encourage the fencing off of upland streams, reducing cattle and sheep access and allowing trees and plants to grow

It is quite remarkable the amount of 'fiction dressed up as fact' that has been written over the centuries about the migration of the salmon. Of Howlett's contribution, only the fact that they spawn "*in the latter end of the Year*" is correct. Adult salmon do not feed in fresh water and they do not go to sea "*to be purged from the Gross Humours*", like overweight humans spending a fortnight in a health-farm.

Even the sensible Mrs. Beeton repeated some wild claims in her *Book of Household Management*, 1859-61:

"*Dr. Block states that gold and silver rings have been attached by eastern princes to salmon, to prove that a communication existed between the Persian Gulf and the Caspian and Northern Seas, and that the experiment succeeded.*"

While the good Mrs Beeton's recipes for cooking salmon are excellent, salmon have never travelled to the warm waters of the Persian Gulf!

A most fascinating piece of science fiction – or, to be generous, mad hypothesis – came from the great salmon-angler, Richard Waddington (*Salmon Fishing*, 1959). He considered that smolt migration was intimately linked with the spawning of the Atlantic eel (*Anguilla anguilla*) in the Sargasso Sea, south of Bermuda at 29°N 64°W, and the migration of larval eels, known as 'leptocephali', from the Sargasso to the shores of Europe.

The marine feeding ground of the salmon, he wrote, "*must be in the cold water of the Arctic or it must be in the warm current of the Gulf Stream...We cannot rule out the former possibility, but it seems not so probable as the latter...in spring, the salmon deserts the continental shelf and rising to the surface finds himself in the warm waters of the North Atlantic Drift. With the natural reaction of all migratory creatures...he swims against the current...he immediately encounters the leptocephalus...as he goes west... the leptocephali he encounters become smaller and smaller... our fish arrives nearly to the eel's spawning places...he must turn round and go home...and follow the stream of larval eels now starting their journey to fresh water.*"

Waddington believed, therefore, that salmon fed on a continuous stream of larval eels stretching from the Sargasso to the shores of Europe. He even devised special fishing 'flies' that imitated eels. That his fishing flies proved to be very successful was purely coincidental. Unfortunately, it only reinforced his belief in a totally erroneous hypothesis. Salmon do not visit the Sargasso to feed on baby eels.

What is astonishing is that the true sub-Arctic feeding ground of the salmon, off West Greenland, had been discovered in 1957 – two years before Waddington's book was published!

How the Oceanic Feeding Grounds were Discovered

It had long been known that the local fisherman of West Greenland occasionally caught salmon when long-line fishing for cod (*Gadus morhua*). It was thought, however, that these salmon originated in Greenland's only salmon river, the Kapisigdlit. Then, in 1953, Jorgen Nielsen examined some scales from these salmon and discovered that they had spent between one and three years in the river as parr. They could not be Kapisigdlit fish, since most of the parr in that sub-Arctic river are four or five years old when they become smolts and head to sea. Clearly they must have come from rivers further south.

In November 1955, an adult hen salmon was stripped of her eggs, tagged and released into Loch na Croic on the west coast of Scotland. Eleven months later, she was recaptured near Maniitsoq, on the West Greenland coast. Four years later, a fish that had been tagged as a smolt in the Miramichi was also captured near Maniitsoq. These were the first recoveries of tagged salmon that demonstrated how both European and North American fish feed in the same Greenland waters.

In the 1960s and 1970s, 4,657 salmon caught feeding off West Greenland were tagged and released. Of 93 recaptured, 28 were recovered in Canadian waters, 44 in the United Kingdom, 16 in Ireland, three in Spain and two in France. In the 1970s, a similar tagging experiment was carried out on salmon caught feeding in the Norwegian Sea. This indicated that the Norwegian Sea was a major feeding ground for salmon originating in the more northern European rivers. Most recaptures were in Norway and Russia, though some were recovered in the United Kingdom.

The feeding grounds around the Faroes (where commercial fishing commenced in the late 1960s) can be divided into a southern sector and a northern sector. Of 1,946 fish tagged feeding in the southern sector in the years 1969-76, 33 were recovered in Scotland, 31 in Norway, 15 in Ireland and eight turned up in other European countries. These had all spent just one winter at sea (1SW). Some returned to their natal rivers as 1SW grilse, but three tagged fish were later recovered feeding off West Greenland. This indicated that after their first year feeding in this southern Faroe sector, those that will eventually return to their natal rivers to spawn as multi-sea-winter (MSW) salmon travel much further after their first year at sea.

Tagging of 5,448 salmon caught feeding north of the Faroes in 1992-5 resulted in only 106 recaptures. Most recaptures were from Norway (47), Scotland (12), Ireland (9) and Russia (6), with fewer from other European countries. There were also four recoveries from Canadian waters showing that, just as European salmon cross to the western side of the Atlantic to feed, so some North American fish travel to the eastern side.

> '*Since the advent of the high seas fisheries off West Greenland in 1957 and off the Faroes and in the Norwegian Sea some years later, much more is now known about the salmon's ocean life...*'
> Derek Mills, *The Ocean Life of the Atlantic Salmon*, 2000

> '*We have scarcely begun to solve the problems of where the salmon feed at sea.*'
> J.W. Jones, *The Salmon*, 1959.

The Departure of the Smolts and the Problems of Adaptation

One of the greatest problems faced by anadromous fish (fish that are born in rivers and then go to sea to feed and grow) is that their physiology – initially adapted to living in fresh water – must cope with the switch to living in salt water.

Like all freshwater fish, salmon parr have body fluids that have higher concentrations of dissolved salts than the water in which they live. Their bodies automatically take in water through the process of osmosis wherever soft thin membranes are exposed, notably the mouth, gills and vent. This water must be excreted, otherwise oedema would eventually result in death. So parr are constantly excreting very dilute urine but retaining essential salts.

As soon as the smolt leaves its river and enters the sea, the problem swings to the other hostile extreme. Ocean seawater has a salt concentration of about 1 ounce per pint (35 grams per litre) of water. This is far more concentrated than the post-smolt's body fluids. Now, the osmotic process is reversed and the fish's body constantly loses water to the sea. If the fish failed to cope with this, dehydration would eventually cause death. To survive, the post-smolt drinks large quantities of seawater. The kidney desalinates this water by removing salts from the blood and retaining pure water, and the fish excretes small quantities of very concentrated urine. The gills are also employed in the excretion of salts.

It appears that smolts from most river systems must reach the sea when the sea temperature is about 8-10°C if they are to acclimatize quickly and move out to sea. If the sea temperature is colder than this, they will either linger in the lower reaches until the sea temperature has risen, or move very slowly out to sea. River flow can also be important, especially in smaller streams. In drought years, with reduced river flow, the downstream progression by the smolts may be slower than in years of normal flow, and result in a later than normal entry into the sea. Any delay in getting out to sea results in higher smolt mortality. This may be due partly to predation in the dangerous shallows of the river mouth, but higher mortality may also be due to the physiological stresses of the fish trying to switch to a saltwater mode though still in fresh water.

Large numbers of smolts will move together under the cover of darkness

The Smolts Move Out to Sea

As smolts move down the river they tend to do so passively, carried tail-first by the flow, mainly at night. In rivers with large estuaries, tagging studies indicate that they also move passively tail-first through the upper part of the estuary as the tide ebbs, also mainly at night. However – and salinity may be the trigger for the change in behaviour – once the smolts reach a certain point in the estuary, they begin to swim actively out to sea no matter what the time of day.

Once they have reached the sea, the young salmon face a new set of problems. They are now called 'post-smolts' and are still only 6-8 inches (15-20 centimetres) in length. It is essential that they do not remain too long close to the shore where predators are numerous. There are also strong tides and a variety of changing currents that could knock them off their course to the distant feeding grounds. To be swept away and carried in the wrong direction by some adverse current could be disastrous. They must get to the prime feeding areas in order to grow and they must do so without delay.

Acoustic tagging of post-smolts in several estuaries has shown that while, initially at least, tides and currents do affect the direction followed by the small fish, they quickly adjust to a course leading to the oceanic feeding grounds. However, a study using hatchery-reared smolts in Trondheim Fjord showed that strong westerly winds blowing directly into the Fjord can significantly delay the departure of smolts.

The abundance of marine food enables the post-smolt to put on weight rapidly after its restricted river diet

To The Oceanic Feeding Grounds

1. North American Salmon

Post-smolts from rivers south of Labrador head north and east to feed in the southern part of the Grand Banks and Labrador Sea with a surface temperature of 4-10°C. They then overwinter in the Bay of Fundy and in a broad area extending around the eastern and southern fringes of the Grand Banks. Having spent one winter at sea, the fish are now 1SW salmon. Some of these return home that summer to spawn as grilse.

Those 1SW salmon that do not return home to spawn head north through the Labrador Sea, into the Davis Strait and Irminger Sea off Greenland. In warm summers, when the sea surface temperature in Greenland fjords rises to 3°C or higher, many salmon feed very close to the shore. When inshore waters are colder than 3°C, the fish remain offshore, south of the 3°C isotherm. A very small proportion of North American salmon swim east from the Irminger Sea to feeding grounds in the Norwegian Sea, north of the Faroe Islands.

These fish overwinter south of the winter pack-ice or to the south and east of the Grand Banks. Most return to their natal rivers the following year as 2SW salmon. Some remain out at sea, feeding through the summer in the same areas that they fed in through the previous summer. They then move south for the winter before returning home to spawn as 3SW salmon (see page 132).

The reduction of the feeding grounds

D.G. Reddin calculated that in March 1969 the area available for salmon feeding in the Labrador Sea/ Davis Strait was some 35,500 square miles (92,000 square kilometres). This was the area of sea with a surface temperature above 3°C but below 8°C. He repeated the calculation for March 1984, and found that the potential feeding area was only 2,300 square miles (6,000 square kilometres).

Because the cooling of the north-western part of the salmon's feeding grounds coincided with a warming further south, the distance separating the 4°C and 8°C surface water isotherms was much narrower throughout 1984 than it had been in 1969. This reduction in suitable oceanic feeding habitat has been blamed as the primary cause of the collapse of multi-sea-winter (MSW) salmon since the 1960s (see also page 18).

Five salmon on the Faroese Banks. Some may return to home waters as grilse, others continue on to Davis Strait (Greenland) for another year of sea-feeding

2. European Salmon

Post-smolts from Spain, France, the British Isles and southern Scandinavia head north to feed around the Faroes and in the southern part of the Norwegian Sea. Fish from Russia and northern Scandinavia go west to the Norwegian Sea. Some Icelandic fish move east to the Faroes and the Norwegian Sea. There appears to be no evidence of any great movement in late autumn into special winter quarters.

After overwintering, a proportion of these 1SW salmon head back home to breed as grilse. Some of the rest move further north into the Norwegian Sea to feed in their second sea-summer, whilst others cross the Atlantic to feed in the Irminger Sea, Davis Strait and in Greenland's inshore waters (but only when the sea surface temperature there is above 3°C). All these feeding grounds have shrunk in area since the 1960s and, consequently, the runs of MSW salmon have been greatly reduced (pages 60-1).

Those salmon that have fed in the north-west Atlantic may spend their second winter at sea over-wintering with American fish, whereas those feeding in the Norwegian Sea drift southwards, keeping to water with a sea surface temperature above 3°C. Most 2SW salmon return home to spawn, though a small proportion may remain at sea, feeding in the same cold waters, for one or two more years.

Some post-smolts, most notably from the Loire-Allier system, head directly across the Atlantic to feeding grounds in the north Labrador Sea, Davis Strait and Greenland fjords. There they remain for two or three summers' feeding before returning to their natal rivers to spawn.

Depth

Salmon at sea tend to stay in the surface 30 feet (10 metres). However, radio-tagged fish have been recorded diving to over 500 feet (150 metres), and certain crustaceans that only live at depths of 1,000 feet (300 metres) or more have been found among the stomach contents of salmon.

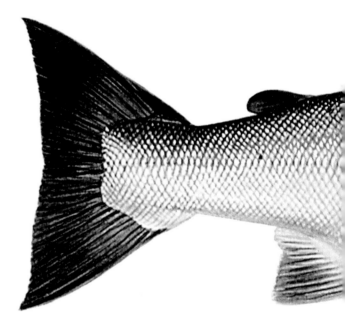

Daily routine

Salmon feeding at sea tend to be more active in daylight hours, and slow down when it is dark. In the salmon's more northern feeding grounds (off Greenland and in the Norwegian Sea) close to the Arctic Circle, day-length is close to 24 hours through the summer.

Swimming speed on the feeding grounds

Tagged fish in the Faroes feeding grounds were recorded swimming at 0.36-1.6mph (0.57-2.5kph).

Schooling or shoaling

Although smolts move down their natal river in shoals and returning salmon can often be seen in large shoals, the fish appear to occur in smaller groups while on the feeding grounds. The post-smolts and older immature salmon from one river do not seem to remain together as they feed.

Small spring salmon (8lbs/4k) from the River Findhorn in Scotland

Filter–feeding

One usually thinks of a feeding salmon chasing and grabbing relatively large prey fish. In fact, the larval sand-eels taken by post-smolts are often only 1 inch (2.5 centimetres) in length and very slender. Other larval fish and many of the crustaceans taken by post-smolts from the surface plankton are also tiny.

These prey are often too small for salmon to hunt individually. Instead, the salmon swims through the shoals of larvae its with mouth open. As the water containing the larvae passes into the mouth and out through the gills, the gill-rakers filter out the food which is then swallowed, Gill-rakers are stiff spines on the side of the gill-arch, opposite the oxygen-absorbing gill-filaments.

Feeding at Sea

As post-smolts head out to sea, they immediately switch from their insect-dominated river diet to a marine diet. This is based initially on crustaceans and other tiny invertebrates. Once the post-smolt reaches about 8 inches (20 centimetres), lesser fish become increasingly important items in the diet. These fish-foods are mostly larval or very juvenile fish, which drift almost passively, feeding off other plankton that are concentrated in the surface layer of the sea. Salmon are 'opportunistic feeders' when at sea and will probably eat whatever food creature is available, provided that they can swallow it.

Maximum size of prey

Salmon do not bite pieces off their prey or masticate their food. The maximum size of prey is determined by the maximum diameter of prey that can be swallowed whole. This is equivalent to about 2-2.5% of the length of the salmon itself. As the salmon grows, so it is capable of swallowing larger prey.

Thus, an 8" (20cm) post-smolt is capable of swallowing a prey 0.2" (5mm) in diameter, whereas a 20" (50cm) fish is capable of swallowing a prey 0.5" (12.5mm) in diameter.

The diet of post-smolts as they head northwards from France, Spain, the British Isles and Fenno-Scandia is often predominantly larval sand-eels*, herring and blue whiting. For post-smolts heading into the Norwegian Sea from Russia and northern Fenno-Scandia, the dominant food is larval red-fish (also called Norway haddock). The major fodder-fish for post-smolts feeding on and around the Grand Banks are capelin and American sand-eels. In Icelandic estuaries and inshore waters, post-smolts also eat large quantities of three-spined sticklebacks.

Timing is vital

The post-smolts must reach the area in which these planktonic fish larvae may be found at a time when they are abundant and also small enough to be swallowed. It they arrive too soon, the larvae may not have hatched. If they arrive too late, the prey may have grown too large to be swallowed. By arriving spot on time, the post-smolts can gorge themselves on the larval fish. Then, as they grow themselves, so the post-smolts can continue to feed on the growing prey fish. The bigger the post-smolt, the less the risk of being eaten by predators. Thus, when the post-smolts grow very quickly mortality is lower than when food is scarce and growth slow.

* Scientific names of marine foods are given on pages 58-61.

Grilse running into the River
Halladale on a flood tide

Marine Food

Fish

Sand eels (*Ammodytes tobianius*, *Ammodytes marinus*, *Ammodytes americanus*, *Hyperoplus lanceolatus*) are amongst the most important sea-foods of all salmon.

Herring (*Clupea harengus*) are widespread in the salmon's ocean range.

Sprat (*Clupea sprattus*) may be important in inshore waters around the British Isles and the English Channel and are a major food (with herring) of Baltic salmon.

Blue Whiting (*Micromesistus poutassou*) are especially important as food for post-smolts travelling north-east off the Outer Hebrides.

Red-fish (*Sebastes marinus*) migrate north into the Barents Sea in summer and mating occurs there in autumn. The eggs are not actually fertilized until late winter (the sperm are stored in the female's body until then), by which time the red-fish population has migrated southwards into the Norwegian Sea. Live young are produced in May-June in the seas around the Lofoten Islands, close to the north-west coast of Norway, at precisely the time that post-smolts are migrating through the area.

Capelin (*Mallotus villosus*) occur in the Norwegian Sea from Trondheim Fjord northwards and around Iceland, Greenland and the Canadian coast (especially the Grand Banks). Capelin frequently spawn in very shallow water (often on beaches among breaking waves) in vast numbers. They are especially important food for salmon around Greenland and the Canadian coast.

Lantern-fish (*Myctophum punctatum*) is a deepwater species up to 5 inches (13 centimetres) long, with

a huge mouth and luminous organs on its ventral surface. They are found throughout the Atlantic.

Barracudina (*Paralepis coregonoides*, *Notolepis rissoi*) is another deepwater fish, up to 16 inches (40 centimetres) in length, found throughout the Atlantic away from the Continental Shelf.

Pearlsides (*Maurolicus muelleri*) is a deepwater species up to 2.5 inches (6.5 centimetres) long with luminous organs on its body. Though widespread across the Atlantic, it mostly features in the diet of salmon in Faroese waters.

Cod (*Gadus morhua*) Larval cod may be important in the diet of salmon feeding over the Grand Banks; they have also been recorded in salmon caught in Greenland waters.

Three-spined Stickleback (*Gasterosteus aculeatus*) Anadromous sticklebacks have been found in the stomachs of juvenile salmon feeding in Icelandic waters.

The importance of fish in the salmon's diet

Many studies have shown that fish comprise the bulk of the salmon diet: on the Grand Banks 98% by weight; in the Labrador Sea, Davis Strait and inshore Greenland waters 82-83%; around the Faroes 66% and in adult salmon returning home through waters around the British Isles 99%. The rest of the salmon's diet is made up mainly of crustaceans.

The flesh of salmon is orange or pink because of the carotenoids obtained from crustaceans, even though they comprise a relatively small part of the diet. Salmon are capable of retaining even minute quantities of carotenoids.

The capelin, an important food for salmon, found around Norway, Iceland, Greenland and Canada

Bottle-nosed dolphins (*Tursiops truncatus*) have been filmed catching and tossing the corpses of dead salmon into the air in the Moray Firth, Scotland

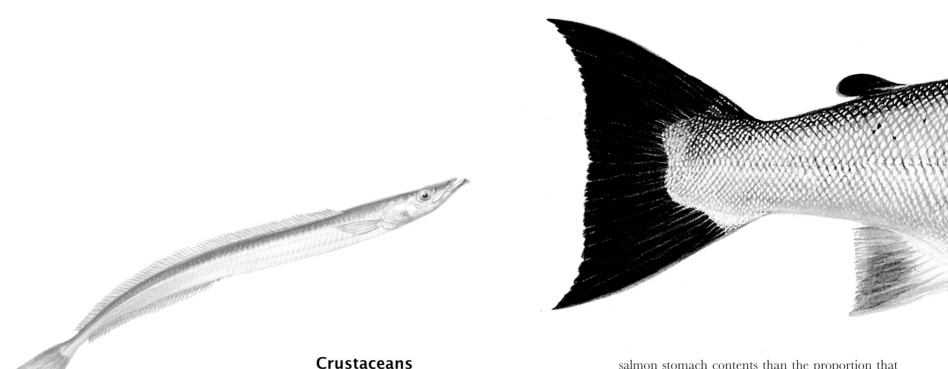

The Sandeel: one of the most common and widely spread sources of food for the salmon

Crustaceans

There are so many species involved that it is, perhaps, simpler to consider the three major groups taken by salmon.

Amphipods These small shrimps have laterally flattened bodies and are the most important group of crustaceans eaten by salmon. Amphipods comprise 87% of the crustacean component of the salmon's diet on the Grand Banks, 97% in the Labrador Sea and up to 97% in Faroese Waters. There is evidence that salmon prefer amphipods and may feed on them selectively. Samples have shown a higher proportion of amphipods to other crustacea in salmon stomach contents than the proportion that occurs in the plankton at large.

Isopods These small shrimps have dorsally flattened bodies. They are commonly found in salmon stomachs in the Norwegian Sea.

Euphausiids These are the famous 'krill' of Arctic and Antarctic waters and are important in the diet of salmon around Greenland, the Norwegian Sea and the Faroes.

Brown Shrimp (*Crangon crangon*) 340 brown shrimps were found in the stomach of an adult

A perfectly-conditioned grilse returning to the river after one winter at sea

salmon caught in the North Sea off Northumberland in 1976. This is cited merely to show that, generally, salmon are opportunistic feeders and will eat what nature puts in front of them.

Molluscs

Snails and bilvalves (notably the edible mussel *Mytilus edulis*) have been recorded from the stomachs of salmon feeding in estuaries.

Squid (*Gonatus fabricii*) Squid often feature in the diet of salmon in the Labrador Sea/Davis Strait area and in the Norwegian Sea.

The feeding season at sea

The main feeding and growing season is spring, summer and early autumn. This coincides with maximum productivity of the surface layers of the North Atlantic. The amount of food consumed by salmon declines quickly by mid-autumn, possibly because less food is available. In one study in the Labrador Sea, 28% of stomachs were completely empty in autumn. Feeding rate is very low in winter; a study in November-December found 47% of stomachs empty, whereas in spring only 8% of stomachs were empty.

The Food of the Returning Adult Salmon

'During the homeward migration the feeding activity of the Atlantic salmon tends to cease.'
Jan Aarge Jacobsen & Lars Petter Hansen in D. Mills (ed.), *The Ocean Life of the Atlantic Salmon,* 2000.

Insects as a food of salmon at sea

Parr and smolts regularly eat winged insects from the water surface when they are in the river. It seems that this fondness for flies persists even after salmon have gone to sea. Post-smolts have been recorded taking land-bred flies which have drifted far from land, from the sea surface. This has been observed off the Hebrides, in the North Sea and in Norwegian inshore waters. Even more remarkably, grilse have also been seen taking flies out at sea on their journey home after a year at sea.

Whilst on their oceanic feeding grounds, salmon become fat, their protein-rich muscles containing large quantities of energy-rich oils. These stores of 'fuel' are accumulated in the tissues so that the fish can return to their home rivers and spawn successfully. If food was scarce on their return journey, more energy might be expended in trying to find and capture such a scarce resource than could be gained in its consumption. Yet if a food source was readily available, it would seem strange for the salmon not to take advantage of it. In a study of salmon returning to Icelandic rivers in September, not one had any food in its stomach, though the last part of their journey had been through shoals of juvenile pollock (*Pollachius virens*) and three-spined sticklebacks. In contrast, another Icelandic study found 30% of salmon had food in their stomachs (mainly herring and sand-eel).

In the 1890s up to 48% of the stomachs of salmon entering the River Tweed contained food in the form of herring, then abundant in the North Sea, into which the Tweed flows (see also page 68). More recent studies have yielded the following results:
• In Norwegian home-waters, only 10% of stomachs contained food; mainly herring, sprat and sand eel.

• Off the West of Scotland, 13% of stomachs contained food (mainly sand eels) in spring, but by early July, all stomachs of returning salmon were empty.

• Of salmon taken off the Labrador Coast in August, 86% of the stomachs contained food. 60% of which was amphipod crustaceans and 25% sand eels.

• Of adult salmon caught in the Gulf of St. Lawrence, only 14% had food in their stomachs - mainly capelin and sand eel.

• All of a sample of salmon returning to rivers draining into Ungava Bay had empty stomachs.

It seems that while there is a general reduction in feeding by returning adult salmon, clearly some will take food if it is available.

Grilse crossing the Shelf Current and approaching shallow water on their homeward journey

Summer grilse from
the River Hallidale, Scotland.
Grilse can vary subtly:
some shorter and fatter, others
more long and slender

Growth at sea

Size is usually recorded in either weight or length. In the past, weight was the prime measure, since salmon sold commercially for food are always sold by weight. However, as catch-and-release of salmon is becoming an integral part of rod-and-line fishery management (page 127), and because it is essential that a salmon should not be lifted out of the water if it is to survive after being released, weighing is being superseded by measuring the length of the fish in the water.

At the end of the first winter at sea, juvenile salmon have grown up to about 18 inches (45 centimetres) in length. Many of these will return to their home rivers as grilse. Before they do, they spend further time feeding at sea. The longer they remain at sea, the larger they will be when they return. Grilse returning in May and June to many of the Irish rivers average about 4lb 8oz (2kg), whereas grilse returning to many other rivers in July and August may average about 7lb (3kg), while those returning in October will be up to 11lb (5kg).

Most of those salmon that remain for a second full summer at sea may return just before or during the following winter, or at the end of winter without further significant feeding. On the Loire-Allier system, they are referred to as two-sea-summer fish and average about 10lb (4.5kg). These are, in fact, the same class of fish as the famous 'spring salmon',

so prized on some of the large Scottish rivers (notably the Aberdeenshire Dee). These fish have an average weight of around 9lb (4kg). Incidentally, 'spring' is something of a misnomer here, for in January and February the snow may be lying deep on the banks and the rivers running with miniature icebergs and soupy ice 'grue'. Some of those fish that are caught in what is really winter may well have run in November, before the previous year's fish have spawned. They may spend a year or more in the river before spawning.

Those fish that spend two summers and two full inters in the sea return as 2SW fish. They will usually feed for part of a third summer before returning. The more food they consume, the larger they grow. A 2SW salmon returning in June may weigh 11-13lb (5-6kg), whereas a fish that returns in September or October may have grown to 15-24lb (7-11kg), or even larger.

Some salmon remain out at sea for the entire third summer and a third winter. Most of these run in autumn at weights often in excess of 30lb (13kg). (see pages 70-71)

Stunted Salmon

In recent years, when feeding conditions for 2SW and older fish have been very poor, scale reading has shown growth-checks in a small proportion of fish. In other words, for a period of time during the main feeding and growing season, these fish have not been able to find enough food to maintain growth. The late 1990s also produced some record small salmon. In June 1998, I caught a grilse weighing 1lb 8oz (0.6kg) in Ireland's River Mourne and in July of that year, I witnessed Alan Davies catching a 1lb 8oz (0.7kg) grilse on the Spey.

The marine predators of salmon

'... *salmon are rare dietary items of marine fishes, mammals and birds.'*

W.A. Montevecchi & D.K. Cains
in D. Mills (ed.), *Salmon at the Edge*, 2003

The Grey seal has increased tremendously in numbers in recent years. It is inconclusive whether they damage salmon stocks significantly

Stocks of Atlantic salmon have declined since the 1970s whereas the populations of several potential predators have increased in the same period, especially grey seal (*Halichoerus grypus*), harbour seal (*Phoca vitulina*), harp seal (*Phoca groenlandica*) and the gannet (*Morus bassanus*). Superficially, it seems easy to link cause with effect: an increase in predator numbers resulting in a decline in salmon stocks. Yet are the two really linked so simply in that way? To what extent does predation by sea mammals and birds affect the population of the salmon? We know that in the river and estuary predators often take a large proportion of juvenile salmon. Do predators take a high proportion of salmon stocks out at sea?

In one of the earliest studies (1958-71), 361 grey seal stomachs collected off the Scottish coast were examined. 27% contained some salmonid remains. Further research was carried out based on the analysis of grey seal faeces. This failed to find any trace of salmonid remains. Why the staggeringly disparate results? The 1958-71 samples were of seals shot close to nets set to catch salmon. The seals had been attracted to easy food in the form of netted salmon (in the same way, seals try to break into the cages of salmon farms). When salmon are not already trapped, however, the evidence suggests that seals rarely catch them.

Studies of harbour seals gave similar results: 18% of seals shot close to fishing-nets off Scotland in 1956-71 had recently eaten salmon, whereas under 3% of faecal samples contained salmonid remains. Another study concluded that, "*salmon are rare or*

absent in the diet of harp seals". In yet another study, the remains of only two salmon were found in 8,000 seal stomachs. Nevertheless, in 1996 one estimate suggested that throughout the Atlantic waters off Canada, seals consume 'probably in the order of 3,300 tons [3,350 tonnes]' of salmon (D. Mills, ed., *Salmon at the Edge*, 2003).

In May 2002 a workshop organised by Ireland's Loughs Agency entitled Seals/Atlantic Salmon Interaction revealed that, as far as Irish waters were concerned, "*salmon was not recorded in either faecal or stomach content analysis...Although local fishermen cite seals as major predators of salmon...no salmon remains were found in any of the samples.*" This workshop demonstrated that seals take a wide range of other marine fish species that are all probably easier for seals to catch than salmon.

Despite the above evidence, opinion amongst fishery biologists appears to be that the impact of seals on salmon populations is grossly underestimated by recent studies. It is argued, for instance, that seals eat only the soft parts of a salmon and discard the head and the skeleton. Thus, no evidence that a salmon has been eaten can be found in the faeces. Further research is being carried out on this topic.

The Harp seal, a species which has been witnessed chasing salmon in Arctic waters. In this illustration they are feeding on capelin

Huge salmon and their demise

I mention several times in this book how oceanic climate changes in the last quarter of the twentieth century have greatly reduced the marine feeding areas of Atlantic salmon and how this has brought about a decline in stocks. This has especially affected MSW salmon which feed in the northernmost parts of the marine feeding grounds. The post-1970 decline of MSW fish (mostly 2SW and 3SW) was not, however, the first population decline to be observed. Even in the bountiful 1960s, 4SW and older salmon were very rare. It seems that there occurred an earlier decline in stocks of 'huge' salmon. From the few of these that have been scale-read, they were fish of 4SW and 5SW (for scale reading, see pages 82-85).

Fortunately, from the point of view of this researcher, salmon anglers in the British Isles have always been keen to keep records. From these records, published in a variety of journals, magazines and books and also details from private papers passed on to me by generous correspondents, I have been able to produce a long list (page 70) of huge salmon. These are fish that weighed in excess of 50 pounds (22.7 kilograms) and were caught by both net and rod-and-line. Today, Atlantic salmon over 40 pounds (18.2 kilograms) are 'as rare as hen's teeth'. In the past, however, 40-pounders were relatively common. The capture of many went without being properly recorded, if they were recorded at all.

For instance, Robert Pashley, the 'Wizard of the Wye', caught 29 salmon of between 40 and 48.5 pounds (22 kilograms) from just two beats on the River Wye.

On page 71 there is a list of salmon in excess of 60 pounds (27.3 kilograms) caught from Norwegian rivers. I cannot pretend that it is anywhere near complete. It seems that at one time, Norwegian 50-pounders were too numerous for them all to be recorded. In one visit to lodges in the Gaula valley, I traced three unrecorded 50-pounders and there were six from the Namsen valley. Visiting the Bolstad River in the summers of 1920-39, C.M. Wells caught twelve salmon of over 50 pounds.

Elsewhere in Europe we have few records. The huge salmon from the Rhine (page 71) must surely only have been one of many. Currently, one of the best areas for catching mammoth salmon is the Baltic, where the populations of prey species such as herring and sprat have exploded in recent years.

Although some Canadian rivers have reputations for producing 'big' Atlantic salmon, I have traced only three 'huge' ones from Canada (also listed on page 71).

Perusal of these records shows that the 1920s was the peak decade for these enormous salmon. This is the clue as to where the huge salmon have gone. Up to the middle of the twentieth century, the North Sea had an enormous stock of herring. We know that salmon fed on herring in the North Sea. In a very early study, conducted in 1894, 43.5% of spring salmon netted in the lower Tweed had herrings in their stomachs. In 1895, 48% of adult salmon taken in spring out in the North Sea had herring in their stomachs. Subsequently, in the second half of the twentieth century, the herring stocks collapsed and this coincided with the disappearance of huge salmon from the catch records.

It is interesting that when North Sea herring stocks were thriving there was also a fishery there for the enormous 'tunny', or Atlantic bluefin tuna (*Thunnus thynnus thynnus*). These fed exclusively on herring. In 1932, Col. E.T. Peel (of the British Tunny Club) caught a tunny of 789 pounds (359 kilograms). In 1933, L. Mitchell-Henry caught one that weighed 851 pounds (387 kilograms).

Are the crash of herring stocks, the loss of the big tunny, and the disappearance of huge salmon in rivers draining into the North Sea or its proximity, mere coincidence?

A shoal of grilse on the Faroese Banks

Some of the largest salmon recorded in the British Isles

WEIGHT	DATE	RIVER	CAPTOR	NOTES
103lb	1901 or 1902	Devon	–	Netted
84lb	1869	Tay	Wullie Walker	Netted
82lb 14oz	1881	Eden	–	Netted
72lb	–	Tay	–	Netted
70lb	1870	Tay	–	Netted: 53″ long, 31″ girth
70lb	1872	Tay	–	Netted
69¾lb	1743	Tweed	Lord Home	Doubts as to how this fish was weighed
67lb	autumn 1812	Nith	Jock Wallace	It took 10 hours to land this fish
65lb	1922	?	–	Found on a fish–stall in London
64lb	7 October 1922	Tay	Miss Ballantyne	Caught by harling; the official rod–caught record
63½lb	1905	Wye	–	Netted
62½lb	1899?	Tay	John Haggart	Spinning with Phantom Minnow
62½lb	1908	Tay	–	Netted
61½lb	October 1907	Tay	Mr Stewart	Worm
61½lb	March 1924	Exe	–	Netted
61lb	late 18th century	Tweed	Lord Home	
61lb	March 1870	Tay	J. Taggart	Spinning with natural minnow
61lb	15 July 1890	Taw	–	Netted
61lb	July 1924	Don	–	Netted
61lb	21 October 1924	Deveron	Mrs Morrison	The British record fly–caught salmon.
60lb	1907	Tweed	–	Found dead on bank
60lb	1888	Eden	L. Bridges	England's record rod–caught salmon; on fly
60lb	1934	Usk	–	Netted; rod–caught record salmon for Usk 48lb in 1913
59½lb	12 March 1923	Wye	Miss Doreen Davey	Devon minnow; a 4SW fish, 52″ length
59lb	October 1888	South Esk	Mr Somerville	
58lb	1872	Shannon	–	Not known whether rod–caught or netted
57½lb	October 1886	Dee (Aberdeen)	J. Gordon	One account gives this as 56½lb and dated 1888
57½lb	27 October 1886	Tweed	Mr Pryor	Weighed 60lb when caught; Silver Wilkinson
57½lb	1907	Tay	–	Netted
57½ lb	1937	Tay	Mr Bainbridge	
57lb	spring 1874	Suir	Mr Michael Maher	On home–tied fly, the Mystery
57lb	1888	Annan	–	Netted
57lb	8 October 1909	Awe	?	Fly
57lb	8 July 1921	Awe	Major A.W. Huntingdon	On Mar Lodge; the Major also has a 51lb fish in the list!
57lb	1967	Tay	?	
56½lb	1909	Tay	–	Netted
56½lb	1944	Tay	–	Netted
56lb	c. 1880	Eden	Mr Francis	
56lb	November 1892	Eden	G. McKenzie	
56lb	1903	Lune	–	Netted
56lb	1913	Usk	–	Netted
56lb	31 October 1920	Deveron	Col. A.E. Scott	Fly: 1/0 Britannia
56lb	12 June 1923	Awe	H.T. Thornton	Fly: size 5/0. Mr Thornton also has a 51lb fish in the list.
55½lb	28 September 1898	Tay	Capt. A.G. Goodwin	Spun minnow (but prawn according to one reference)
55½lb	October 1903	Tay	P.M. Coates	Fly: Wilkinson; Mr Coates also had 51lb fish in same month!

Salmon flies, with gut
eyes and exotic feathers and furs,
were considered essential for catching
salmon on rod and line at the end
of the nineteenth century.

British and Irish records of 50lb+ salmon by decade

Pre-1861	1861–70	1871–80	1881–90	1891–1900	1901–10	1911–20
5	2	10	17	3	20	11
1921–30	1931–40	1941–50	1951–60	1961–70	Post-1970	
37	9	4	0	3	0	

Norwegian salmon over sixty pounds

Unlike the British and Irish list (above), this is likely to be far from complete. The pattern of dates is, however, of interest!

WEIGHT	DATE	RIVER	CAPTOR	NOTES
79.38lb	July 1928	Tana	H. Hendrickson	The World rod–caught record!
76lb	July 1921	Aaro		In Bergen Museum
74.97lb	July 1925	Dramens		Netted
73.87lb	1878 or 1879	Tana	'A magistrate from Utsjok'	
73.86lb	June 1923	Sulen		Netted
71½lb	1927	Vosso	Herr Denissoff	
69½lb	1921	Aaro	J. Aarven	
69½lb	June 1924	Namsen	S. Kjolstad	A 4SW fish
68.56lb	November 1919	Vosso		Netted
68½lb	1924	Aaro	Herr Denissoff	
68.2lb		Bjora		
68lb	1923	Vosso	Herr Denissoff	What a great trio the man had!
65lb	June 1920	Vosso	F. Isdahl	Mr Isdahl caught a 47lb fish the same day
64lb	1929	Aaro		
64lb	June 1961	Vosso		
63lb		Sand		
61lb	1924	Bolstad	H. Charrington	
60½lb	1965	Vosso	O. Haraldsen	Spinning or prawn?
60lb	1929	Alta		
60lb	1929	Vefsen		
60lb	1951	Alta	Lord Dudley	

Fourteen out of nineteen records are from the bountiful 1920s!

A Huge Salmon from the Rhine

In March 1866, the fishery scientist Frank Buckland found, in a London market, a salmon that had been caught in the Rhine. It was a male, weighed 69.5lb, was 4′ 8″ (1.4 metres) long and had a girth of 2′ 6″ (0.75 metres). Pollution later wiped out the Rhine population of salmon.

Two Mammoths from the Baltic

9 May 1995, 60.5 lb (27.48kg), Bay of Pukavik, Baltic Sea
10 April 1992, 58lb (26.36kg), Bay of Pukavik, Baltic Sea

Three big salmon from North America

They were all from the Cascapedia river:
1.   54lb caught in 1886 by a Mr Dunn
2.   54lb caught in 1920 by a Mr Nadean
3.   53lb caught in 1892 by a Mr Stanley

There is Still Hope!

In 1993, *Trout & Salmon* magazine reported that the largest Atlantic salmon ever taken on the fly had had been caught that year on the Varzina, on Russia's Kola peninsula. This huge fish, measuring 57.5 inches (1.44 metres), was caught and released by Sir Seton Wills. Such a fish would have weighed in excess of 70lb (30kg). There are reports of other monsters being caught in Russia, but without accurate weighing and measuring, they cannot be accepted as a record. Nevertheless, it offers hope that, one day, we will see these huge salmon again.

CHAPTER FOUR

RETURN TO THE RIVER

'They ascend the Rhine to the falls of Schaffhausen, and go up by the Aar into the lake of Zurich.'

H.G. Seeley,
The Fresh-Water Fishes of Europe, 1886

O ne of the most remarkable features of salmon behaviour is their ability to leave a relatively small river estuary, to range across vast tracts of ocean, and then to return, not only to the river of their birth, but to the very stretch of that river where they were born.

Evidence for this comes from some quite simple experiments. The first was by P.D.H. Malloch, who marked smolts in the River Tay with fine silver wire rings; 1.7% were caught after returning to the Tay.

In 1992 W.M. Shearer reported a neat experiment in which eggs from the River Conon were raised in a hatchery supplied with water from the River Garry. The fish were then tagged and released as smolts in the North Esk. The tagged fish that were caught on their return were all from the North Esk; not one was reported from Conon or Garry.

In a Swedish experiment carried out in the 1960s, B. Carlin collected some fertilized ova from the River Angermanalven and raised them to smolt stage in a hatchery. The smolts were then put in a cage which was placed in the River Ume for one month and then in the River Lule for one week. The smolts were tagged and half were released into the Lule and half into the River Kalix. Of the smolts released into the Lule, 150 were later caught as adult salmon in the Lule, but six found their way back to the Ume and one to the Kalix. Furthermore, while

74 of the Kalix contingent found their way back to the Kalix, three were caught in the Lule and three in another river, the Torne.

These experiments show that most salmon find their way back to the river they left as smolts. Most, but not all salmon return to their home river: perhaps 95%. But what of those that 'get lost'?

If all salmon returned to their home rivers, few rivers would have salmon. Ten thousand years ago, almost all present-day salmon rivers were in the grip of the last Ice Age. When the Ice Age ended and northern rivers flowed once more, they were colonised by salmon that had failed to return to the rivers they left as smolts. The salmon now running the great rivers, like the Restigouche and Miramichi, Spey and Tay, Namsen and Alta, are all descended from fish that 'got lost'.

Similarly, in more recent times, rivers that lost their salmon stocks through pollution in the 19th and 20th centuries, and have subsequently been 'cleaned up' have been recolonised quite naturally by 'lost' fish.

In 1913, Augustus Grimble wrote that "*the Mersey, Calder and Weaver…are absolutely ruined.*" Since 1980, over £1billion has been spent on cleaning up the foetid Mersey Basin. In 2002, 26 'lost' salmon tried to recolonise it.

An alder–lined nursery stream flows beneath snow–covered hills. A juvenile salmon will spend at least one, maybe two, years here before going out to sea

How do salmon find their way around the oceans and then back home?

The easiest way to answer this is to compare the salmon's methods to those by which human beings can find their way: orienteering, navigation and piloting (or homing). The three methods are similar, but subtly different. All three might be used simultaneously, or only one may be used. It is important, however, to remember that humans use each of these consciously. Observations and measurements are taken before changes in direction are made. With the salmon the whole process is unconscious; it is instinctive or automatic. The salmon does not 'make a decision'. It does not think or analyse and then decide the direction to take. Which is why its migrations are so wonderful.

ORIENTEERING
Orienteering is a sport in which competitors find their way around unknown countryside using only a map, a compass and visible landmarks. Is it possible for salmon to orienteer their way around the North Atlantic? Do they have a map and a compass, and what seamarks might they use?

The map may be produced by the salmon themselves, in their brains, as they move out from the river in which they were born. Or they might be born with the map already in place as a genetic inheritance. We don't know which.

There are plenty of seamarks that could be used and added to the map as they travel. The North Atlantic has a complex coastline, with many archipelagos and submarine ridges. There are also distinct bands of current that salmon either follow or head into; for instance, the North Atlantic Current, the Shelf-Edge Current, the Irminger Current and the Labrador Current. Furthermore, salmonids have been shown to be able to detect changes in salinity of less than 0.15mg sea-salts per pint or 500 millilitres (sea water contains 1 ounce per pint or 35g per litre). Thus slight fluctuations in salinity, related perhaps to proximity to estuaries or to melting pack-ice, may be useful seamarks. The varying sea temperatures that salmon swim through, or the position of the 3°C isotherm that they will not cross, might also provide seamarks.

But what of a compass? The compass that we would use involves an iron needle that points to the Earth's magnetic North Pole. With it we can take a very precise bearing.

T.P. Quinn demonstrated that sockeye salmon responded to the Earth's magnetic field. If the field was shifted by 180° the sockeye turned and began to swim in the opposite direction. In 1980 K.P. Able made the crucial point that, "*for magnetic-compass orientation the animal must have some sort of paramagnetic material…or deposits of permanently magnetic material in its tissues.*" Then in 1990 A. Moore, S.M. Freak and I.M. Thomas reported that they had located magnetic iron particles in the lateral lines and head of the salmon.

We now have the compass; the body of the salmon. As it moves through the ocean the salmon's body can detect changes in current, salinity and sea temperature, and note headlands, rocky skerries, islands and underwater ridges. When it is essential that a change of direction be made, the salmon does not have to look at map and compass and think. Automatically the change of direction is made, by muscles and skeleton linked to lateral line and head through the coordinating nervous system of the fish.

Recently, adult salmon returning to their home rivers have been found to be following distinct compass bearings that will take them home…or almost home.

Ghostly images: salmon moving with the tide in a silt-laden estuary

NAVIGATION

Navigation is not the same as orienteering, but complements it. In navigation, which is the method used by ocean-going sailors to keep a fixed course, a compass, a calendar, a chronometer that keeps accurate time, and a sextant to establish the position of the sun are all needed. After taking simple readings with these, it is easy to calculate the precise position of a ship.

We have already noted that salmon contain magnetic iron in their lateral lines and head: they have a compass. But what of calendar and chronometer, and what about the position of the sun?

A calendar is determined by changes in day-length throughout the year. Most plants and animals living in northern temperate and sub-Arctic regions respond to changes in day-length. Snowdrops begin to flower before crocuses, which begin to flower before daffodils, which begin to flower before tulips. Each of these blooms at a certain day-length in spring. They can tell how long the day is to within a very few minutes. They have a calendar. So have salmon.

The salmon's chronometer, like that carried by so many other animals, is based on the progression of the day, perhaps using the position of the sun in the sky. Though we carry watches, we too have a similar natural chronometer. Look at how we carry out certain functions at almost precisely the same time every day without looking at a watch!

So how does the sun help to fix a position? Birds that migrate at night, such as thrushes and warblers, use the major constellations as their guide. Should they be en route when a bank of cloud obscures the night sky, they may be pushed off course by the wind and make landfall far from their intended destination. Salmon also use the sun's position. They can detect its altitude in the sky and, when thick cloud obliterates the sun, they can sense its polarized light rays as they pass through the cloud.

So salmon can navigate, and do so accurately. By having also the ability to orienteer, their route around the North Atlantic is precise; as precise as a long journey you might make in your car – provided you don't take a wrong turning and get lost! When they are out at sea, salmon do not get lost. It is wrong, as some have done, to describe their travels as 'wanderings', for that suggests a nomadic journey on an unplanned route. A salmon at 59°N 38°W and heading due west knows precisely where it is: following the Irminger Current on its way to the Davis Strait after a summer's feeding on the Faroe Bank.

Sea–silver salmon pausing
at the river mouth before nosing
into fresh water

HOMING OR PILOTING

Orienteering and navigation can take a salmon around its North Atlantic domain and back, close to home. The last part of the journey calls for great precision so that the salmon can end its journey in the part of the home river where it was born. This final homing is through the process of piloting, in which the salmon follows a signal sent out from its final destination. It is rather like a fishing boat I was once in, beyond the sight of land on Lake Ontario. The boat automatically piloted itself back to harbour in Cobourg, following a radar beam sent out from the harbour. Or it is like the aeroplane in mid-Atlantic that flies to JFK Airport on autopilot following a beam sent by JFK to that aircraft.

It seems that each river, and each tributary of each river, has its own taste or smell. Somehow, juvenile salmon learn the smell of their own river or tributary just as they leave it as smolts. Parr that have grown up in one river, but are later released as smolts in another river, will return to the latter river. Parr raised in a river but then released out at sea as smolts do not return to their home river. It seems that they do not learn its 'taste' unless they actually swim down the river as smolts. Experiments have also shown that smolts which have had the nerve linking the olfactory lobes (the ones that detect 'taste' or 'smell') with the brain severed, cannot find their way home.

We do not know for sure what the taste of a salmon's own river actually is. Some evidence indicates that geology, agriculture, land use and land type in the river catchment all contribute to that river's unique scent. It has also been suggested that parr living in a river may release some sort of pheromone (a chemical messenger) that passes out to sea. Each river population of parr might have their own particular brand of pheromone so that a salmon returns to its own related population. This might explain why salmon will often home-in to a tiny tributary in which they were born. There may be something in the pheromones produced by the parr living in that tributary that says: 'Come back here, for you are one of us!'

Thus the salmon completes its journey to the river of its birth.

That rivers have their own taste or smell and that salmon are piloted back to their home river by that taste or smell is not a new idea:

'Doubtless, to the fish each river has got its own smell... When I see an old gentleman sniffing at the tops of port wine decanters I always think of Salmo salar looking for his own river.'

Frank Buckland,
Familiar History of British Fishes, 1873

Post-smolts heading out to sea. Memorising the taste of their home-river will enable them to return

How long do salmon stay out at sea?

TELLING THE AGE OF A SALMON

Early in its life, scales grow from scale-buds to cover and protect most of the body of the salmon fry. The number of scales on the salmon remains constant (or almost so) throughout its life. Occasionally, scales are lost and, when they are, new 'replacement scales' grow quickly to cover the tiny areas of exposed skin. As the fish grows from a little parr to a huge salmon, the size of each scale increases, but the number of scales stays unchanged.

Scales do not grow at a constant rate. Rings of new material, called *circuli* are laid down around the edge of each scale. Because salmon grow far more quickly in summer than they do in winter, the summer *circuli* are much wider than the winter

Replacement scales

When a scale is lost, so too is the record that it held. A replacement scale that has grown on the body of a smolt will lack all parr *annuli*; there will be an area of fairly constant growth, with sea summer *annuli* to the outside formed when the fish was a post-smolt. Similarly, a replacement scale that has grown on the body of an adult salmon at the end of its first winter at sea will have an area of constant growth (the record of its parr and first summer and winter sea-life will be missing) with wide second-summer *circuli* to the outside.

ones. Thus, one set of wide summer *circuli*, with a set of winter *circuli* to the outside, shows one year's growth of both scale and salmon. By counting these bands – called *annuli* – we can ascertain the age of the fish.

When a salmon is feeding at sea it grows much more rapidly than it did as a parr in the river. By looking at the very narrow *annuli* in the centre of a scale we can read the number of years the fish spent in the river. There may be only one of these narrow *annuli* in a fish that spent only one year in the river as a parr. By counting the much wider *annuli* (outside the narrow river *annuli*) we can tell the number of years the fish spent in the sea.

When a salmon returns to fresh water, growth stops in both body and scale. From the scale, we can often read when the fish stopped feeding and returned to fresh water. If, for instance, a salmon caught in July shows no growth at all after the *circuli* of the previous winter were laid down around the edge of the scale, we know that it stopped feeding and returned to the river before spring, probably in March or April.

When a salmon prepares for spawning (page 21), tissue around the edges of the scales is re-absorbed by the body. If we look at the scales of a kelt, they appear eroded. If the kelt makes it back to sea, feeds and then returns to the river, the new growth on the scale appears around that eroded edge. The eroded edge, with new growth outside is called a spawning mark. Some kelts return to the river to spawn for a second time the autumn after their previous

spawning, so that we see only wide summer *circuli* outside the spawning mark. Others remain out at sea for a full year or more before returning. In such fish, we will see a completed *annulus* (sometimes more) of wide summer *circuli* with narrow winter *circuli* on the outside.

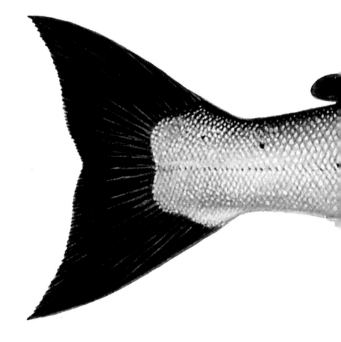

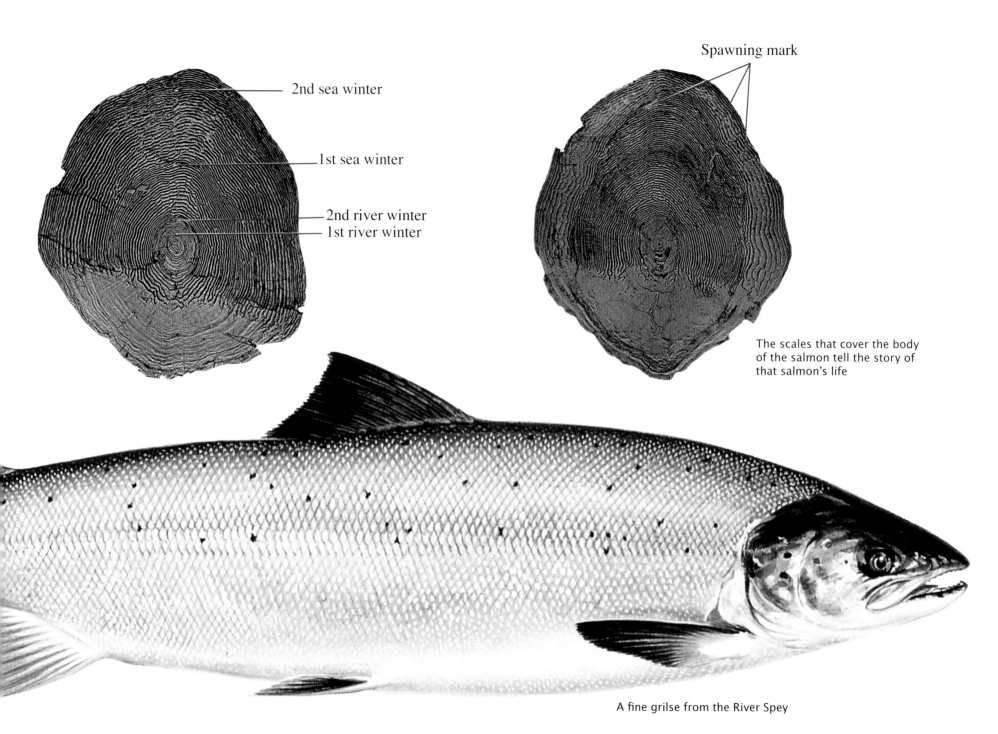

2nd sea winter

1st sea winter

2nd river winter
1st river winter

Spawning mark

The scales that cover the body of the salmon tell the story of that salmon's life

A fine grilse from the River Spey

What scales can tell us about the age of salmon on their first return from the sea

Different rivers, or rivers in distinct regions, often have their own age-ranges of salmon. These may be different from the age ranges of salmon from other rivers or regions. Parr grow more quickly and go to sea earlier in some rivers (warmer, southern ones) than others (see page 38). That is largely a consequence of different rates of growth in the rivers. Once at sea, however, all salmon feed, in general, in the same feeding grounds. Since the opportunity to feed and grow is the same in any given feeding ground, differences in the age at which salmon from different natal rivers return to spawn may be genetically determined.

River Loire–Allier
The majority of juveniles produced by this very long French river system go to sea after one or two years in the river. About 25% return after two summers feeding at sea and 75% after three summers at sea. Fewer than 1% return as 1SW grilse.

Rivers Sella and Eo (Northern Spain)
Around 70% of parr from these rivers smolt after one year, the rest after two years in the river. About 75% return as 2SW salmon, 15-20% as 3SW salmon and only 5-10% as 1SW grilse.

Corrib and Foyle systems (Ireland)
60% of the juveniles smolt after two years in the river, about 32% after just one year and fewer than 8% after three years. About 90% return as 1SW grilse and 10% as 2SW salmon.

Rivers Ribble and Lune (NW England)
Most juveniles smolt after two years in these rivers, most of the rest after three years, with only a small proportion after one year. That has not changed in the past 50 years. What has changed, however, are the proportions of different sea ages of returning salmon:

In the 1960s and early 1970s, about 25% returned as 1SW grilse, 60% as 2SW salmon and up to 15% as 3SW salmon.
In the 1990s and early 2000s, about 65% returned as 1SW grilse, 35% as 2SW salmon and fewer than 1% as 3SW salmon.

North Esk River (Scotland)
The majority of juveniles go to sea after two or three years in the river. In recent years, about 70% have returned as 1SW grilse, 30% as 2SW salmon and fewer than 2% as 3SW salmon, with some very rare 4SW fish. As in the Lune and Ribble, 1SW grilse formed a much smaller component of the runs in the 1960s.

River Tana or Teno (Norway/Finland)
Most juveniles go to sea after three to five years in the river; the full range is two to at least eight years. Up to 60% return as 1SW grilse, the other 40% being divided up into 2SW, 3SW, 4SW and 5SW categories of virgin salmon (salmon that have not previously returned to spawn)

The rivers of Quebec (Canada)
Most juveniles smolt after three or four years of river life, the maximum range being one to at least five years. Most return as 1SW grilse and 2SW salmon, with a very few 3SW fish.

The rivers of Newfoundland
As in the Quebec rivers, most juveniles smolt after three or four years of river life (range one to at least five years). About 75% return as 1SW grilse, 22% as 2SW salmon, 3% as 3SW salmon and fewer than 1% as 4SW.

Shafts of evening light penetrate a deep holding pool on the River Tyne, England

What scales tell us about salmon that return to spawn more than once, and about very old salmon

G.A. Nall recorded one of the oldest hen salmon ever caught. She was thirteen years old when caught in Scotland's Loch Maree. She had already spawned four times and was on her fifth spawning run. But she had not spawned every year. Instead, she had taken a full year's break, feeding at sea and recovering from the previous spawning, before returning to fresh water.

A hen salmon, weighing 52 pounds (23.7 kilograms), caught in the Sundal River (Norway) in 1928, showed a similar pattern. She had first run the river and spawned as a 3SW fish. She then spent a year at sea before returning to spawn, and then had another year at sea before being captured on her third spawning run.

In recent years, a small proportion of the salmon population of the River Tana/Teno (Norway/ Finland) has been discovered to have a similar multiple spawning strategy. The virgin fish, with up to eight years in the river and five years sea-

feeding (see page 82) behind them, return to the river and spawn in late autumn. They then spend the winter in the pitch dark, close to freezing-point, beneath the ice covering the river. Come the spring melt, they head out to sea for at least one full year before making their next spawning run. Those that survive their second spawning, over-winter beneath the river ice before heading out to sea – again for at

least a full year before making their third spawning run. This relatively small number of multiple-spawners have been estimated to attain weights in the 44-66 pounds (20-30 kilograms) range. Some of them, therefore, fall into the category of 'huge salmon' (see pages 68-71). Potentially, they may be a great age: perhaps 8+ parr, plus 5SW salmon on their first return to the river. With another two

A salmon from the River Aros on Mull. Short rivers like this on the West coast of Scotland have a higher proportion of multi-spawners than those elsewhere

spawning years, taking a year off at sea in between, such fish would be 17 years old.

In contrast, many other kelts get back to sea in winter or early spring; feed for only a few months, then return on their second spawning-run the following autumn.

Repeat-Spawners

In the 1930s, over 30% of all Newfoundland fish were repeat spawners. Generally, however, up to 10% of salmon running short rivers are repeat-spawners, fewer than 5% in long rivers (1% in the Loire-Allier). The vast majority of repeat-spawners are females.

How to identify a repeat-spawner:
1. Its scales will have spawning-mark(s).
2. It will have gill-maggots attached to its gill filaments (as do kelts and some virgin fish that have been in the river for some time)
3. It tends to have more black spots on its gill covers and head.

The timing of salmon runs

In the Loire-Allier, the timing of the run of salmon is dictated by water temperature and condition in the extremely long lowland stretch between Nevers and the sea. This stretch is inhospitable to salmon from late spring through to the first floods of autumn – by June the water temperature here may have reached 28°C. To avoid the high summer water temperatures in this stretch, the salmon run from about October to late April or early May, the larger three-sea-summer (3SS) fish tending to run earlier than the 2SS fish. In contrast, the short rivers flowing north from the Cantabrian Mountains in r fish tend to run earlier than smaller, younger fish.

In the far north, the timing of salmon runs is again dictated by temperature In this case, the rivers have to be free of ice so that the fish can run. In the rivers of Kola, Finnmark (Tana and Alta Rivers) and Iceland, and in the cold rivers draining into the western Atlantic from the north east United States and Canada, ice melt may not occur until April or May. Here, the fish run from late May or June through to autumn (August-October). Older, larger fish tend to run early (on the Alta and Tana in June and July), with grilse dominating the run from mid-July through August, and with a later run of older, larger fish in late August and September.

The British Isles are almost unique in that fish can be found running somewhere or other on any day of the year. On some Irish rivers (e.g. Lennan, Drowes), the fishing season begins on January 1 when fish will be running the river. Scottish and other Irish rivers open on dates in January, February and March, whilst some rivers in the English West Country close their fishing season in December. Thus, on almost any day of the year, a fresh-run salmon may be caught legally somewhere in the British Isles. Larger rivers (e.g. Dee, Spey, Tay, Tweed, Foyle) have more prolonged and varied runs than short rivers, and runs can be divided into three categories:

1. Spring run

This run is mainly composed of 2SW salmon and lasts, according to tradition, until 30 April or 31 May. The run often begins in early winter (November onwards), with fish accumulating in the river before opening day. These fish run and spawn the following autumn furthest up the river system. This component of the annual salmon run has declined greatly in some large rivers (notably the Aderdeenshire Dee) in recent years, though in the Tyne, England's most prolific salmon river, the spring run is a dominant feature.

2. Summer run

Consisting mainly of 1SW grilse with a few larger 2SW fish, this run peaks through June and July, provided river flow is satisfactory. The summer run dominates the salmon population of most Irish rivers.

3. Autumn run

This run peaks from September through to the end of the season and consists of a mix of ages including 1SW grilse and MSW salmon, including repeat spawners. This run now dominates the salmon populations of many smaller rivers (e.g. Nith and Annan, Derwent, Ribble and Lune) that in the 1960s had also a spring and summer run.

A pod of summer-run salmon. Some rivers have summer runs, others do not

Hormones and salmon migration in the river

Hormones may be described as 'chemical messengers' secreted into the blood system from endocrine glands, which evoke various responses around the body. The hormone insulin, for instance, is produced by just a few cells called the Islets of Langerhans in the pancreas. Insulin causes all the cells in the body to take glucose from the blood, and the liver to absorb and store excess blood sugar. In salmon, release of the hormone thyroxine by the thyroid gland causes increases in heart rate, in energy production in the muscle tissues and in alertness.

M. Fontaine found that levels of thyroxine were significantly higher in migrating salmon. This might be expected, since the salmon needs a higher heart rate to supply oxygenated blood rapidly to its hard-working muscles when actively swimming in the ocean or running upriver to its spawning grounds. It also needs a heightened alertness so that it can avoid predators and negotiate the obstacles on its journey.

When a salmon reaches the lie in which it will be resident for a number of weeks (in spring-run fish, possibly many months), it is important that its thyroxine level falls. When it has reached its resident lie, the salmon no longer needs to expend as much energy as it did while migrating. Indeed, it must now conserve its body's resources until they are needed for the rigours of spawning.

A working sketch of three grilse, jostling for position in a favourite lie

Thyroxine and the salmon angler

Salmon that have been in the river for some time are said to be 'stale' or 'potted'. They have low thyroxine levels and are often very hard to catch. Fresh run fish have higher thyroxine levels; they are more alert and more likely to take the angler's lures. Generally speaking, the longer a salmon has been in the river, the lower its thyroxine levels and the harder it is for the angler to catch.

Anglers used to 'awaken' stale fish by throwing rocks into the river, or by letting the dog go for a swim across the pool. A convoy of canoes passing through will also sometimes do the trick. Such tactics probably work (when they do) by causing a temporary rise in thyroxine, making the fish alert to perceived danger or disturbance.

Knowledgeable fishers are also aware that stale fish will often take a fly in the evening. As the light begins to fade, fish that have been in the pool all day may be ready to move upstream at nightfall. Their thyroxine levels rise and so too do their energy levels. They become more alert and, again may be more responsive to the angler's lure.

Temperature and its influence on salmon entering the river from the sea

Salmon tend not to run into a river from the sea when the river water temperature is less than about 4°C or greater than about 22°C. The former is more likely to restrict entry in winter and early spring, or during the start of ice-melt in northern rivers. The latter commonly applies during the summer, in rivers towards the south of the salmon's range – Quebec southwards, central Fenno-Scandia and the British Isles southwards. High river temperatures are usually associated with very low river flows during hot, prolonged droughts. Salmon that are ready to enter the river are already under stress, with a physiology switching from living in salt water to fresh water (see also page 48). They must minimise further stress by avoiding high water temperatures and the hazards of running very shallow, drought-stricken rivers.

Salmon held up in the sea by high river temperatures and low flows wait for a cool spate in order to enter the river. It seems, however, that protracted waiting is itself physiologically stressful and may result in high mortality.

In wet years, with good river flows throughout, salmon can run from sea to river whenever they are ready, and overall, salmon runs tend to be larger than in 'dry' years of prolonged drought.

In southern rivers, where long hot summers are the norm, such as the Loire-Allier, runs are timed to occur when the river water temperature and flow are optimum (late autumn to early spring).

Salmon are cold-blooded

This is not strictly true. More correctly, salmon are 'poikilothermic' animals. This means that they are unable to regulate their body temperatures in the way that mammals and birds can. Instead, their body temperature is determined by that of their immediate environment – the water in which they swim. The rate of all metabolic processes – the myriad of chemical reactions occurring in all cells of the body – are temperature-related. Within the temperature range in which a salmon can live, the higher the temperature, the faster the metabolic reactions proceed. As a rule-of-thumb, a 10°C increase in temperature results in a doubling of the rate of metabolism. A salmon living in water of 5°C has only half the energy of one in water of 15°C.

It is because they are poikilothermic that salmon feeding at sea will not enter water colder than 4°C (post-smolts) or 3°C (salmon that have spent at least one year at sea). Below these temperatures, energy production would be too low for the salmon to swim in order to feed, grow and survive. At the other extreme, at above 10°C, it seems likely that the metabolic processes work too rapidly for efficiency in salmon that are seeking food. It could be that they burn up more energy at these higher temperatures than they can fuel with the food they catch, or some deleterious product(s) of metabolism may supervene. At sea, then, salmon are forced by their metabolism to waters of between 3-4°C and 8-10°C.

The same metabolic restriction determines the salmon's entry into the river and its upstream migration (see pages 96-97).

Major salmon lies like this one may hold fish that ran the river in early Spring and also fish that arrive in October. The coloured salmon are the stale fish, and the silver specimens are the new arrivals

Tides and wind and their effects on salmon entering the river

Salmon gather off the river mouth. As the tide flows, they advance into the river mouth or through the estuary. Whether any will actually run upstream into fresh water depends on three factors: river water temperature (pages 96-97); river flow rate and the height of the tide.

More salmon tend to run on spring tides, especially those pushed higher up the estuary by strong onshore winds, than on neap tides. Spring tides are the highest tides, coinciding with new and full moons. Neap tides are much lower and coincide with the half moon.

It appears that the shoal of salmon will follow the tide close to its upstream limit, and may run up into the river if conditions are favourable. If conditions are not favourable for running, they will swim back to the sea on the ebb tide.

Two personal observations

Having spent several nights with professional salmon netsmen, who set a trammel-net across an estuary channel and follow it downstream on the ebb, it is clear that more salmon are caught on a spring tide when the river is in a summer drought than on any tide when the river is cool and with a good flow. Under these optimal conditions for catching salmon, most enter the net from upstream (these are fish heading back out to sea having failed to run the river). A high proportion of salmon caught in the estuary during a long hot drought will have lost their pristine silvery sea-colour. This would indicate that they have been passing in and out of the estuary on two tides per day for some weeks.

One August afternoon, we saw about 300 grilse gathering off the mouth of Northern Ireland's River Bush as a spring tide pushed into the sea-pool. The river upstream was very low, and the water warm. As the tide peaked, we observed three fish running through and, as the tide fell, the rest of the shoal vanished into deeper offshore water.

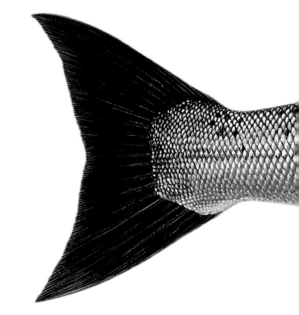

Spring salmon, from the
River Tyne, England, in prime condition

Rain, river height and upstream migration

On some big rivers, such as the Tay and Tweed, Namsen and Tana, and Miramichi and Restigouche, salmon are able to run even during a drought. There are also rivers that have a large lake at their head, which will keep the river flows and levels sufficiently high (and temperatures low) for salmon to run even during a drought. In most rivers, however, salmon will not run upstream during a drought when the river is very low. In these rivers, salmon runs are linked to spates following heavy rain.

After weeks of dry hot weather, a typical spate river will be running very low: 'showing its bones', as anglers say. The salmon in the river will have been in for some time and will be 'stale and potted', in angling parlance. Eventually, after prolonged heavy rain, the river suddenly begins to rise. As the level rises higher and the spate increases, the water becomes dirty with soil washed out of the surrounding land. All sorts of debris get washed away from the bank and are swept downstream: trees and branches; leaves and grass; plastic fertiliser sacks and the odd dead sheep or cow. The river is now a filthy brown flood and its main flow is inhospitable to salmon.

After the rain has stopped, the spate starts to decline. At first, the amount of water-borne rubbish reduces. Then the level starts to drop and the amount of suspended silt, clay or peat material decreases. Shingle banks that had been covered by the flood begin to be exposed again. It is in this latter stage of a clearing spate that salmon start to

run upstream, and they will continue running until the river falls back to its 'normal' summer levels. Apart from precipitation, the rate at which spates may rise and fall is affected by a number of factors, including gradient and topography and the nature of the land in the river's catchment area. Depending on these factors, it may take days or weeks for a spate to clear. Changes in land management and drainage in a river catchment area may radically alter the spate pattern of a river. In rivers where formerly a spate might have taken weeks to clear, it may now take only a matter of days as a result of changes to land drainage.

Analyses of thyroxine levels in salmon caught in the River Tay at Perth and in Girnock Burn (a tributary of the Dee) found that - up to a certain point - the higher the river flow rate, the higher the level of thyroxine. At very high flow rates, however, the thyroxine levels in salmon were actually lower.

We can now relate thyroxine levels, river flows and the upstream migration of salmon. When the river is very high, in a filthy flood, salmon will not run. Instead, they move out of the main flow into sheltered spots and rest, and their thyroxine levels fall in order to conserve energy. However, as the spate clears and conditions for running improve, thyroxine levels in the salmon increase. Then, as the river approaches low summer levels again, the salmon stop running upstream. They take up resident lies and their thyroxine levels fall again to conserve energy.

The record bag of salmon

Grimersta is a chain of five lochs on the Hebridean Isle of Lewis connected to the sea by the one mile (two-kilometre) long Grimersta River. There are man-made weirs between the lochs that hold back the flow of water through the system. When lots of salmon can be seen off the river mouth, the lower weir can be removed to create a small artificial spate that encourages the fish to run to the first loch. By manipulating weirs further up the system, the run of salmon can be moved further up the system, whilst fresh arrivals can be brought in at the bottom. On 23 August 1888, A.M. Naylor caught 54 salmon that had been induced to run up the Grimersta, as described. It remains the largest one-day bag of Atlantic salmon, to a single rod, from British waters and perhaps anywhere in the world.

Heavy autumn rains on uplands result in a spate in the river and a chance for the salmon to move upstream rapidly

Water temperature and upstream migration

Salmon find it difficult to swim through fast, turbulent white water, to pass up steep fish-ladders, and to leap weirs and waterfalls when the water temperature is below 5°C. At such low temperatures they are unable to generate the necessary energy.

Even at temperatures slightly above 5°C some obstacles may be impassable. The Falls of Cassley, on the Cassley River in north east Scotland, provide a fascinating example of this. The Falls comprise a series of pools separated by waterfalls, each of which requires a minimum temperature before salmon can advance upstream. The lowest, the Round Pool, can be attained from the lower reaches of the river when the water temperature is 5°C, but the passage upstream to Cemetery Pool cannot be made until the water has reached 7°C. Salmon cannot continue from Cemetery Pool to Falls Pool until the water temperature has reached 9°C, and the passage from there into the upper reaches of the Cassley cannot be achieved until water temperature has got to 11°C. The four steps through the Falls require an increasing amount of energy and thus slightly higher temperatures.

When salmon move upstream
Except when the river is 'coloured' – tinged with peat, or holding clay or silt in suspension – most upstream migration occurs between dusk and dawn, though obstacles such as weirs and waterfalls are passed in daylight hours. Salmon that have been resting in a deep pool through the day will often be seen leaping in the pool neck in the evening, preparing for their onward journey. Of course, when the river is very low, upstream progress may be hindered if not completely prevented.

In September 1994, as the light began to fade, I watched salmon moving into the neck of a pool on the River Nith. The river was low, and the run to the next pool very shallow. A few smaller grilse splashed their way through, but all the larger ones moved back into the deeper water as night fell.

In low water conditions, anglers will sometimes catch salmon that have forced their way upstream through very thin water. Such salmon often have visible abrasions on their bellies, caused by the sharp rocks over which the fish have had to squeeze in making their way upstream.

Upstream migration: strategies
Radio-tagged salmon have been found to swim upstream at speeds varying from 3-6mph (5-10kph) where there is no barrier to progress, such as shallow rapids, weirs or waterfalls. Running salmon will, however, pass such obstacles in a matter of minutes, perhaps after a short rest and a few trial runs. If a salmon maintained these speeds, it could reach the headwaters of a river 60 miles (100 kilometres) long in a matter of 10-20 hours. In practice, this does not occur: salmon take much longer to run upriver to their final destination on the spawning grounds.

2SW and older salmon that enter a large river early in the season tend to run far upstream fairly quickly. One radio-tagged fish that entered the Spey in April ran upstream for 50 miles (80 kilometres) in ten days before it took up residence in a lie close to the mouth of a major tributary. In contrast, later run fish tend not to run as far upstream. Radio tracking of another Spey fish that entered the river in summer showed that it ran only 6 miles (10 kilometres) in seven days before it took up a resident lie. It is clear that only a part of the time taken on these initial upstream journeys – perhaps less than five percent – was spent in swimming upstream. The rest of the time is spent resting. Once the fish have completed this initial run and become resident in a lie (see page 98) they seem to switch off; their thyroxine levels fall very low and they will not move unless disturbed, perhaps by a spate or by a predator. Even after they have been disturbed, 'resident' salmon will usually return to the same lies.

Grilse (1SW salmon) appear to show a similar pattern to older fish: those running a large river in May-June will tend to run quickly upstream and further than those running only a few weeks later, in July-August. One grilse tagged in the mouth of the Spey on 24 June took 14 days to run 50 miles (80 kilometres) upstream to its resident lie. Another Spey grilse, tagged on 12 August, took a resident lie only 9 miles (15 kilometres) upstream after three days.

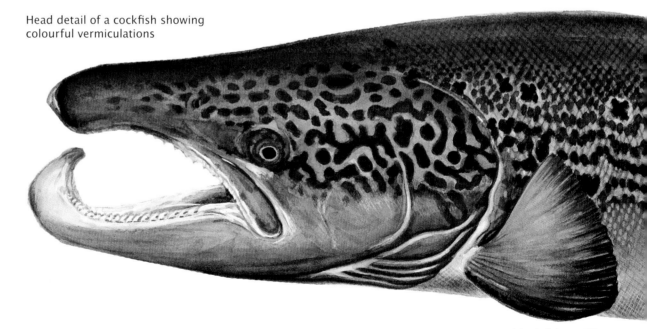

Head detail of a henfish in spawning livery

Head detail of a cockfish showing colourful vermiculations

Resident lies are not usually in the same part of the river where the salmon will eventually spawn. Resident lies tend be in quite deep water, whereas salmon actually spawn in gravel-bedded shallows. Many salmon spawn in tiny streams where it would be dangerous for them to rest for more than a few days. Just before spawning, salmon make a final spawning run that takes them from their resident lies to the spawning areas. The previously mentioned April-run tagged Spey fish ran a short distance from its resident lie into the tributary. The summer-run fish travelled just a short distance further upstream into gravel shallows. In contrast, both of the aforementioned grilse made final spawning runs of 25 miles (40km) that autumn.

The head of a returning salmon holds the sense organs used to find its way home. The olfactory lobes can 'taste' the water; the eyes can record day length and angle of the sun. The skin can detect temperature; the lateral line, down each side of the body, can detect temperature and pressure (currents and river flows). But the salmon does not think or reflect on what these organs detect. Its brain analyses and makes the body respond automatically. No concious decision is made, no thought process involved.

Salmon lies

Salmon usually have three sorts of lie, though there is some degree of overlap between them:

Resting lies are lies used by salmon that are running upstream, where they rest temporarily between bouts of swimming. The easiest of these to identify are those immediately above sections of the river that the fish have to work hard to get through. The tail of a pool immediately upstream of a turbulent rapid, or the quiet water immediately upstream of a waterfall or weir are typical resting lies in which fish will remain for a few minutes before moving on. Salmon making their way up a long shallow riffle will often pull in for a rest beside a particularly large boulder or shingle ridge, just off the main current. These particular lies may be used by several salmon in succession during a run. These lies clearly have some special quality that appeals to the fish, since other apparently similar boulders are completely ignored. Salmon in these resting lies give the angler the greatest opportunities, for they are running fish merely resting for a moment. Their thyroxine levels are elevated, they are in a state of alertness and they are often responsive to the angler's lure.

Resident lies are those which salmon may occupy for several weeks or months, resting in a torpid state while awaiting the final run up to the spawning grounds. Whereas resting lies may be in quite shallow water (less than 3 feet or 1 metre deep), resident lies tend to be in deeper water. Typical resident lies include the deep water on the outside of a meander. In this sort of lie, salmon seem to prefer being close to a sheer cliff or beneath overhanging trees. If the bank is undercut, salmon may lie right under the bank, out of sight. The bottoms of deep, very slow, almost featureless canal-like stretches of river are locations also favoured for resident lies. Deep riffles amongst bedrock outcrops or very large boulders are also typical spots for resident lies; salmon appear to prefer resting over rock than sand or fine gravel.

High-water lies are where salmon are forced to rest when the river is in full flood. This may be in very shallow water over shingle banks that are normally high and dry; over grass on flooded fields and in the shelter of what are normally riverside bushes. Once, when the Conwy Valley in Wales was under water, a salmon must have taken to the flooded streets of a village for shelter. It ended up stranded in the pub car park!

Salmon in lakes

When there is a lake on a salmon river, salmon will often treat it as a giant river pool and have their resident lies there. For some reason, salmon in lakes rarely seem to take up lies in deep water, usually preferring water less than 6 feet (2 metres) deep. Consequently, they are usually found close to the shore. Here are some examples. In Lough Melvin, a huge concentration of salmon builds up in Rossinver Bay into which the spawning stream flows, or along the adjacent shallow of a sandy ridge off Garrison shore. In Lough Fern, fish congregate close to the inflowing and outflowing rivers, often in the middle of flooded reedbeds (the reed stems can be seen swaying as the salmon swim through them). In Glen Lough, the fish concentrate along a narrow band of shallow water close to the southern shore and over a gravel fan off the mouth of the inflowing stream.

Lough Melvin is an interesting case. Salmon run the 5-mile (8-kilometre) River Drowse that connects the lough to the sea from December, but will not spawn until the following November. Progress through the river and lough is fairly slow and predictable. The first main run in the lough follows the northern shore for 6 miles (10 kilometres) to the Garrison shore, arriving in late February and March. A later run, starting in late March, follows the southern shore of the lough to Rossinver Bay. These first arrivals will then spend eight or nine months in the lake before making their spawning run into the inflowing river.

Do salmon feed on their return to fresh water?

Though food items are only rarely found in the stomachs of salmon caught in fresh water, they may very occasionally be seen to take larger insects such as caddisflies, daddy-long-legs, mayflies and grasshoppers. Salmon are also caught on artificial flies designed to imitate such insects, and on 'baits' such as earthworms and prawns. Some suggest that this demonstrates that salmon actually do feed in fresh water on occasions. Others suggest that salmon feed in this half-hearted fashion out of 'feeding habit', or that memories of their earlier existence in the river as insect-eating parr are somehow reawakened.

On 13 March 2002, Mike Maughan caught a salmon in the Aberdeenshire Dee and discovered - when he came to clean it - that its stomach was crammed with 'food'. He put the stomach in his deep-freeze and then posted it to me. The back (pyloric) end of the stomach contained 35 feet (11 metres) of parasitic tapeworms, while the rest of the stomach contained 229 aquatic nymphs, larvae and freshwater shrimps. There was no sign whatsoever of these food items having been digested (either physically or chemically).

Had that salmon been 'feeding', in the true sense of the word? I suggest not. The purpose of feeding is to get nourishment. I don't believe that that particular salmon had ingested all of those food items for nourishment's sake. My own interpretation is that the irritation caused by the chronic infestation of tapeworms had led to an abnormal increase of thyroxine in that fish. Perhaps the salmon ingested all of those food items in an attempt to ease the irritation. Anyway, it was alert enough to see and grab Mike's fly.

There may, of course, be many other reasons why salmon occasionally take food and other items into their mouths while in fresh water. Arthur Ransome, the famous author of books for children, propounded an interesting theory after watching American GIs chewing gum, while sitting in the foyer of a London hotel during the Second World War. Ransome suggested that salmon 'feeding' in fresh water were doing no more than the equivalent of 'chewing gum'. He argued that just as the American soldier was not actually feeding when he chews gum, neither is the salmon that grabs a fly: it is just going through the motions when a morsel is put right in front of it.

The Irish judge and fishing writer T.C. Kingsmill Moore came up with a different argument. "*Modern man uses his mouth only for eating (apart from talking and kissing which have no interest for fish) and he assumes that when a fish takes something into its mouth the reason is that he wants to eat. This overlooks the cardinal anatomical fact that a fish has no hands. Everything which a man does with his hands, or other animals with their paws, a fish must do with its mouth if it does it at all. The mouth is the only available organ for attack, defence, or exploration.*"

One thing is certain; salmon do not feed when they return to fresh water.

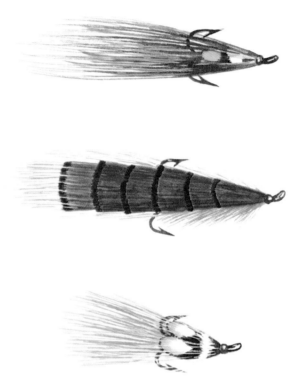

Gaudy, modern salmon
flies like these catch salmon,
despite the fact that salmon
do not feed in fresh water

A salmon pool
on the North Tyne at Countess Park.

Kelt

Death

Almost all cock salmon die after spawning. The long fast after leaving the marine feeding grounds (especially in fish that run in winter, almost a year before spawning); the upstream migration and the rigours of mating require the expenditure of too much energy for the fish to survive. None of the males make it back to the sea. If a salmon loses more than 40% of its body mass, death is practically certain. Few cock salmon lose less than 40%.

The stresses of mating are probably the main reason why so very few males survive, compared with females. Radio-tracking observations by J. Webb and A.D. Hawkins in the 1990s showed that females tend to move quietly away from the redds once they have deposited their eggs and covered them with gravel. Cock fish tend to behave differently. One cock salmon that they followed paired with a hen fish and, after three days of courtship, mated with her. The following day he paired with a second maiden hen and mated with her. He then had a brief liaison with a third maiden hen, but that was not consummated. A few days later, he was observed trying to court a spent hen kelt. After this, he moved downstream and tried his chances with another hen kelt. Moving back upstream, he successfully mated with a maiden hen (no doubt, by this stage, precocious male parr contributed most to the fertilization of the eggs; see page 26). He then courted another hen kelt before dying, exhausted.

Of those salmon that survive a first spawning, get back to sea and return to spawn a second time, almost all are hen fish. Fewer kelts from very long rivers survive to spawn a second time compared with those from short rivers (pages 90-91). Autumn-run salmon are more likely to survive spawning than spring-run salmon, for they do not have to sustain themselves for almost a whole year in the river before spawning.

Surviving spawning involves getting back to the sea and food. One would imagine that kelts will make every effort to make it back to sea. Some do so, heading seawards quickly, immediately after they have spawned. Others, it seems, do not. In April 1991, John Todd and I were fishing the river Bush, in Northern Ireland. We were after fresh-run springers, but caught four kelts which were so emaciated that there was very little between their heads and their tail fins. These fish were unlikely to survive, but were barely half a mile (1 kilometre) from the tide where they might have had some chance of survival had they gone there. Instances have been recorded of kelts surviving in the river until August, and seemingly making no effort to return to the sea.

Salmon that lose over 40% of their body mass before they get back to sea will almost certainly die because their condition becomes so poor that their resistance to infection is severely impaired. They fall prey to various bacteria and the conspicuous white fungus *Saprolegnia*. On seeing a dead kelt covered with fungal lesions, many might imagine that it was the fungus that killed the poor fish. It is, in fact, far more likely that the fungus was a secondary infection and that the salmon would have died anyway.

'And a hundred yards before the Fireplay, Shiner found a kelt with fungus on its head and tail and flank, lying on its side in water not deep enough to cover it. Salar had got so far with the last of its strength, and had died in the darkness.
The spate rose rapidly, and washed all away to the sea which gives absolution, alike to the living and the dead.'
Henry Williamson, *Salar the Salmon*, 1936

Pencil study of the sad remains of a kelt, now food for riverside birds and mammals

CHAPTER FIVE

HAS THE ATLANTIC SALMON A FUTURE?

> *'Salmon are certainly scarcer now than formerly, and the average weight of those taken is much decreased.'*
>
> John Colquhoun,
> *The Moor and the Loch*, 6th ed. 1888

The salmon is often said to be 'endangered'. Indeed, a book by Anthony Netboy, *The Atlantic Salmon* (1968), has the subtitle *A Vanishing Species*. The truth is that the salmon is not an endangered, vanishing species. Certainly the worldwide population of the Atlantic salmon declined between the 1960s and 1990s. Whenever the population of any wild species declines, alarmist conservationists are ready to shout, "It's endangered!" and scientists obtain employment in trying to find ways of solving 'the problem'.

To any true conservationist, the antics of the bird protection industry (especially in the British Isles) are more alarming than the threat to most bird species found in Europe and North America. One recent volume on endangered species, edited by five well-salaried people for Britain's Nature Conservancy Council (now English Nature) and the Royal Society for the Protection of Birds, included such abundant and thriving species as the gannet, whooper swan, shelduck, wigeon, oystercatcher, fieldfare and redwing. Even common birds, it seems, are endangered. But had such species been left out of the book, it would have been a very slim volume. In Britain, there are now more ospreys, peregrine falcons and avocets than there have ever been in historical times and their numbers are still increasing. Yet over a million RSPB members, together with the British government and European Union, remain convinced that they are endangered. Vast funds are made available to protect these spectacular birds – and to pay a lot of salaries.

One of the greatest threats to wildlife is that governments and the public will eventually become inured to pleas for help. Genuinely endangered species may one day be in real trouble if people believe that conservation bodies 'cry wolf' and grab the cash. Thankfully, the organisations most concerned with salmon conservation have not fallen into that trap.

It is true that the world population of Atlantic salmon has declined by perhaps about half since the 1970s. That decline has been mainly amongst MSW fish and it is almost entirely due to poor feeding at sea, especially in the far north of the Atlantic where MSW salmon feed.

Yet we have evidence that the salmon population can bounce back quite quickly. In 2003, the rod-catch on the River Tweed was 13,886 fish. This was over 45% higher than the average annual Tweed rod-catch during the 1990s and close to that of the average Tweed rod-catch of the 1960s.

In 2004, there were actually more rivers with Atlantic salmon than there were 50 years ago. In 2002, anglers declared a catch of 2,585 salmon from the River Tyne. In 1952, the lower Tyne was so grossly polluted that the rod-catch was roughly zero!

The Salmon Factories

Two natural 'factories' are needed to manufacture adult salmon. Both must work at full efficiency if the output of adult salmon is to be maximised.

The River 'Factory'

The river manufactures smolts. Its maximum output is limited because its product (parr that will give rise to smolts) is territorial. Thus, even the most perfect river can produce no more than a certain number of smolts. For that reason, it is pointless to try to increase output in already productive rivers by introducing extra fry or parr from a fish-farm. To work efficiently, a salmon river must have:

1. Sufficient returning adults to procreate in order to produce the maximum population of parr and smolts that the river can sustain: the Conservation Limit (CL).

2. Access to the entire river system for the spawning salmon.

3. Suitable gravel redds for egg laying, that do not silt up, dry out, or become frozen (see page 24).

4. Suitable parr habitat with a mix of gravel and boulders, and both deep and shallow water (see page 32).

5. Sufficient food (insect) production to enable optimal growth of fry, parr and smolts (see page 34).

6. Predator populations that take no more than the surplus parr (those that would be ousted from territories and would die anyway - see pages 40-43).

7. Clean water throughout its course. Many rivers have clean enough headwaters to act as salmon nurseries, but polluted lower reaches will kill any smolts trying to swim to sea and bar the upstream migration of returning adult salmon. This was the problem with the Tyne in the 1950s (see page 105). Its lower reaches were grossly polluted. After they were cleaned up from the 1970s, the Tyne became an excellent smolt factory once more.

If a river's potential as a smolt factory is fully realized, no more can be done. If natural smolt production is less than 100% of potential, it can be boosted artificially by means of hatchery input and smolt ranching.

The Ocean 'Factory'

The second salmon 'factory' is the Atlantic Ocean, where the smolts are 'finished': turned into adult salmon. To work efficiently the ocean 'factory' must have:

1. A maximum supply of smolts from the smolt-producing rivers.

2. A maximum area in which the post-smolts and older fish can feed. This area itself must be capable of producing enough food for the salmon and the other animals against which they compete for food (see pages 12-18, 52-62).

3. Low levels of predation (pages 66-67).

4. The free passage of fish to and from their feeding grounds and also during their sojourn whilst feeding at sea.

We know that the ocean 'factory' is not working at 100%. There is little we can do about oceanic/climatic problems. We can, however, do something about the commercial netting of salmon that intercepts the fish at sea and in the river estuaries.

The rest of this chapter will look at such conservation problems and possible solutions.

Pair of mature salmon

Commercial fishing for salmon

There are three completely different categories of commercial salmon fishing:

1. Capture on the main oceanic feeding grounds.
2. Interceptory offshore netting of adult salmon on their return from the oceanic feeding grounds.
3. The netting of salmon in the estuaries (or lower reaches) of their natal rivers when they return to these rivers to spawn.

1. Fishing on the main oceanic feeding grounds

During the 1970s and 1980s netting of salmon on the high seas was a major source of concern. Today, commercial fishing on the feeding grounds is insignificant.

Greenland fishery

This increased from less than 100 tons/tonnes in 1960 to over 1,500 tonnes in 1965 and to over 2,500 tonnes in the 1970s. Thereafter, annual quotas were agreed and the annual catch declined (often the quota was not reached). Today, the catch is relatively small and goes only for Greenland's domestic consumption.

Faroe fishery

The Faroe fishery began in 1968 with a catch of 5 tonnes, rising to 544 tonnes in 1980 and 1,009 tonnes in 1981, but fell to 672 tonnes in 1985.

Quotas were imposed from 1982 and today the harvest is relatively small.

Norwegian Sea fishery

This fishery peaked at 980 tonnes in 1970, but was closed down by the Norwegian government in 1984.

Those who object to these high seas fisheries on the grounds that they diminish the salmon stocks running their rivers should surely be prepared to compensate the Greenland and Faroese people for not fishing. After all, the post-smolts from our rivers are getting fat in their seas so that we can enjoy having big salmon in our rivers!

Salmon as by-catches

Recently, it has been revealed that significant numbers of post-smolts are being caught accidentally in nets set to catch mackerel, especially in the Norwegian Sea. For instance, in the period 13-17 June 2001, 14 hauls of one mackerel net caught 7.8 tons (7,959 kilograms) of mackerel, and 198 post-smolts and five sub-adult salmon. Steps are being taken to try to reduce this by-catch. One solution might be to lower the fishing depth of the nets to 15-30 feet (5-10 metres) below the surface. This would not greatly diminish the mackerel catch, but it would reduce the by-catch of salmon that generally swim just below the surface.

Otter chasing grilse at the mouth of the River Hallidale, Scotland, on a June night. Although otters do kill salmon, their impact on stocks is negligible. Otters prefer eels to salmon

2. Interceptory netting of salmon travelling back from the feeding grounds to their home rivers

Until very recently, there were three major interceptory fisheries for migrating Atlantic salmon: one off the Canadian coast, another in the North Sea off the coast of north east England, and the third one off the western coast of Ireland. Drift nets were banned from use off the Scottish coast in 1962. Commercial fishing for salmon off the eastern seaboard of the U.S.A. ended in 1948.

The Canadian fishery

The first efforts to close this fishery were made in 1966, but it was not until March 1992 that a five-year moratorium was imposed on commercial netting off Newfoundland, with an offer by the Canadian and Newfoundland governments to buy-out net licences. By the end of that year, 96% of Newfoundland netsmen had accepted the buy-out compensation. In 1993, 60% of the Labrador netsmen followed suit. In 1996, the entire interceptory salmon fishery off the Atlantic coast of North America was closed, with the exception of a small number of fish taken by the aboriginal Innu and Inuit people of Labrador.

The North Sea fishery

Since the 1960s, this fishery, off the coasts of the English counties of Northumberland and Yorkshire, has taken up to 90,000 salmon per annum (the recent average is 33,815 salmon and 35,927 seatrout). These were fish mostly destined for Scottish rivers. In February 2000, a Review Group set up by the UK government presented a report, backed up by a paper, *Interceptory Exploitation of Salmon* by the Atlantic Salmon Trust and North Atlantic Salmon Fund (UK). This argued for the closure of the North Sea fishery, recommending compensation for the 69 licensed netsmen involved.

By May 2003, 22 of the 69 netsmen had accepted the offer of compensation and, by the end of 2003, this net-fishery had been reduced by 80%. By the time that you read this book, the North Sea salmon fishery may be entirely consigned to history.

The Irish fishery

This remains the last significant commercial interceptory fishery for Atlantic salmon, with a declared annual catch of about 2,500 tons/tonnes. These fish are mostly destined for English, French and Spanish rivers. At the time of writing, the Irish government seems not to be prepared to reduce or close this fishery.

Why interceptory fisheries ought to be closed

Interceptory fisheries catch fish destined for many rivers. They do so indiscriminately and deplete stocks in rivers where populations might already be dangerously low. The Irish fishery certainly does prevent salmon returning to rivers that have low populations.

In Tarka the Otter, Henry Williamson describes otters teaching their young to fish. Salmon may be startled and then chased into shallow water where they are easier to catch

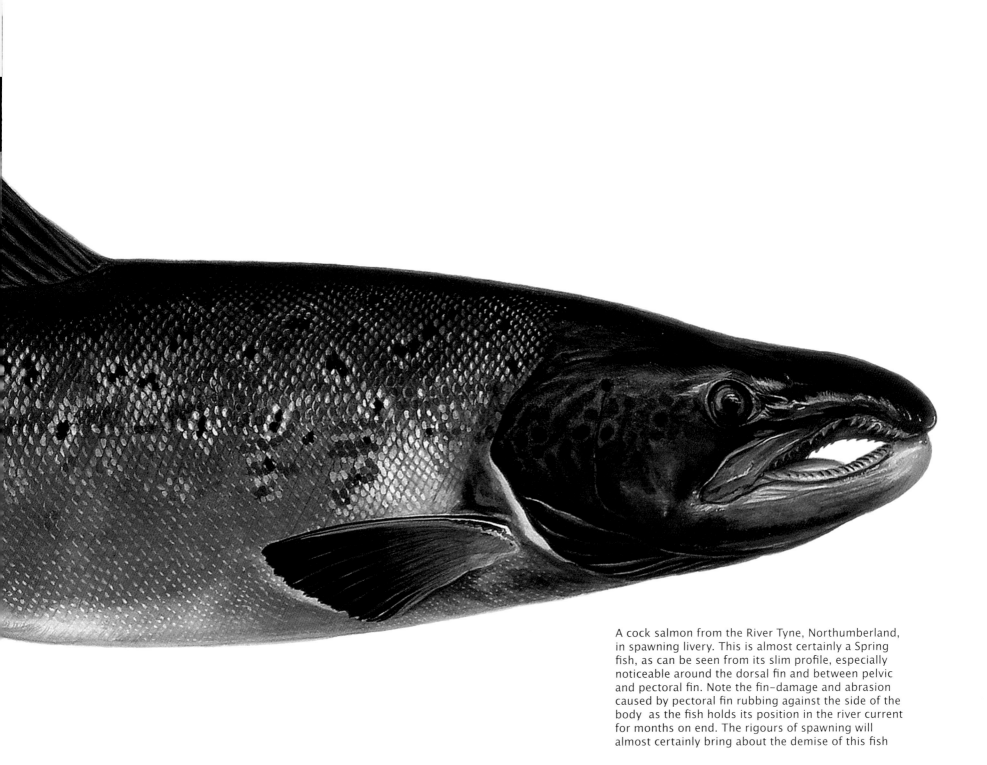

A cock salmon from the River Tyne, Northumberland, in spawning livery. This is almost certainly a Spring fish, as can be seen from its slim profile, especially noticeable around the dorsal fin and between pelvic and pectoral fin. Note the fin-damage and abrasion caused by pectoral fin rubbing against the side of the body as the fish holds its position in the river current for months on end. The rigours of spawning will almost certainly bring about the demise of this fish

3. Commercial fishing in estuaries, and the rod-and-line catch

If a river is producing its maximum number of smolts, and the number of adult salmon returning is greater than the number needed to lay enough eggs to generate the next smolt run (known as the Conservation Limit or CL), then it seems reasonable to harvest the excess. In contrast, where a river is not producing its maximum number of smolts, and the number of adult salmon returning is fewer than that needed to maintain the poplulation (below CL), then it seems wrong to continue harvesting fish until stocks recover to the point that they can generate a surplus. Rationally, this is the only sensible way to manage wild salmon stocks.

There are three main problems. Firstly, most salmon rivers lack automatic fish-counters that can record the number of returning adults accurately. A fish-counter is a vital piece of equipment which allows those managing the river to know whether the CL has been reached, and if it has what harvest of surplus salmon can safely be permitted.

The second problem is that many rivers are greatly under-performing as smolt factories. Much work is needed to improve productivity so that the population of returning adults reaches sufficient numbers to allow sustainable harvesting of the surplus. Simply leaving the river to get on with it and preventing any harvest being taken by net or rod will not be enough. We will look further at this problem later in the chapter.

The third problem is the question of how any surplus stocks ought to be harvested. By nets, or by rods, or both? Angling interests make a powerful argument that the overall economic benefit of a rod-caught salmon far exceeds the commercial worth of a salmon sold for food. Factored into this calculation are the sums spent by anglers on tackle and equipment, the letting of fishing rights, local employment of gillies and keepers, and livelihoods for local pubs and fishing hotels, etc. However, angling, which is a less efficient way of catching salmon than netting, might not take anywhere near the number of fish that are surplus to the CL requirement.

Does that matter? Surely, anglers might ask, a surplus of fish in the river will give us more fish to try and catch with rod and line? In short, better fishing! There is, in fact, a sound conservation argument for estuary nets helping the rods towards harvesting the full CL surplus of returning adult salmon.

When there are too many salmon on the redds, later arrivals often cut into the nests made by earlier spawners. This is wasteful. There is also some evidence that fry production in streams that are overstocked with eggs is lower than in streams that are not overstocked.

Perfect management of a salmon river would seem to involve achieving a balance of harvesting that keeps the rod angler happy (if we salmon anglers are ever happy), but which also utilises net-fishing to ensure that a full sustainable harvest is taken.

The junction pool: salmon will often lie in pools at the confluence of a river and its tributary. From this junction, each fish will be drawn into its natal stream

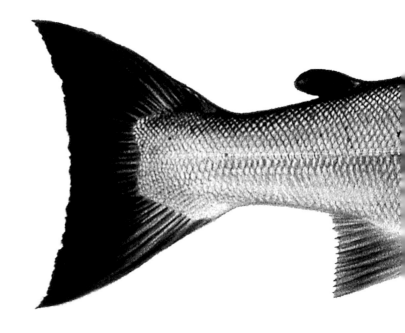

The Foyle system: management of a productive river

The Foyle river system is one of Ireland's major salmon rivers. One tributary, the Finn, has a great spring run of salmon. The other tributaries are magnificent grilse and autumn rivers. The Foyle system is managed by The Loughs Agency, which monitors adult spawning and parr stocks, improves and maintains water quality in the nursery streams, and prevents poaching. Fish-counters immediately upstream of the tide count every returning adult salmon.

The Loughs Agency has calculated that the river requires 8,000 salmon each year to pass upstream of the counter to produce the 9.7 million eggs needed fully to sustain the next generation. In order to achieve this target, the Agency is empowered to close both the net and the rod fisheries if 2,600 returning salmon have not been counted through in the period 1 May to 30 June. Similarly, if 7,000 fish have not passed the counter by 15 September, the rod season can be shortened by ten days (from 20 October to 10 October). So far, The Loughs Agency

has never needed to impose these restrictions, for the numbers have always exceeded these minima. It is a legal requirement that every salmon caught from the Foyle system, whether by rod or net, must immediately be tagged. This has greatly reduced losses through poaching and has provided more accurate records of harvested fish.

Since 1990, the Foyle's average annual net catch (in a six-week season, fishing four or five days per week) is about 35,000 salmon. These are caught in the tidal water. The rod catch has fluctuated in the

range 10,000-12,000 salmon. These are caught in the fresh water of the rivers.

The Foyle is an excellent example of a well-managed salmon river. It combines diligent maintenance of a near-perfect river habitat with the enforcement of sensible regulations which ensure that the harvest of fish does not exceed that which will protect subsequent generations. Alas, many rivers are not of the Foyle's quality, nor as well-managed, and these rivers need to be improved.

The harvest of wild salmon

It is a privilege to eat a wild salmon, whether caught by rod or by net. Those involved with the commercial harvest - netsmen, wholesalers, smoke-houses and retailers - ought to treat wild salmon as a speciality food; a real delicacy. Wild salmon and their products are as 'organic' and 'natural' as any food fish can be. Wild salmon is a fish for the connoisseur and ranks with lobster, turbot and Dover sole. It is a fish deserving of special occasions. Wild salmon should be expensive – far cry from cheap, farmed salmon, which is its pale imitation.

A summer salmon from
the River Coquet, Northumberland, England

The degradation of the river habitat

'Since the beginning of the industrial revolution and the rapid increase in population which accompanied it, the threat to salmon rivers has increased enormously – the threefold threat of obstruction, pollution and abstraction.'

J.W. Jones, *The Salmon*, 1959

Most rivers are not as productive as the Foyle or those that flow through pristine countryside in, for example, Iceland, northern Scandinavia and parts of Scotland and Canada. Rivers that flow close to high densities of human population have invariably suffered simply because mankind has so often abused rivers or used them unwisely.

1. Pollution

Rivers down-wind of coal-burning power stations (as in parts of Britain and southern Scandinavia) have lost salmon stocks through falls of acid rain that lower the pH of the water which leaches toxic aluminium salts from the soil into the river water. The installation of scrubbers that remove sulphur gases from power station emissions can put an end to this insidious form of pollution.

The lower reaches of many salmon rivers are bordered by conurbations that produce vast quantities of toxic effluents; sewage and industrial waste. Traditionally, these have been poured into the river with varying degrees of treatment. Where this pollution is sufficiently bad, it forms a toxic barrier; it kills smolts passing to sea and the returning adults. It was this form of pollution that destroyed the salmon stocks of rivers like the Thames, Rhine, Tyne and Clyde during the 19th and early 20th centuries. In recent times, huge investments have been made in cleaning up toxic effluents and preventing them getting into rivers. These efforts are being rewarded by a return of the salmon to rivers that have not seen them for decades.

Agricultural pollution

Rivers flowing through farmland often suffer from three forms of pollution:

a) Toxic farm slurry and silage liquor
These can leak into rivers if containment measures fail, or if heavy rainfall causes accidental overflows. They can de-oxygenate the water, killing all fish and most insect life.

b) Nitrate and phosphate fertilizers
Fertilisers leaching into the water from riverside fields are an insidious form of pollution. They encourage the development of 'blooms' of algae, especially blanket-weed *(Cladophora)* which clothe the riverbed in summer and autumn. During warm evenings the algae use up oxygen in the water, and oxygen levels may fall so low that parr and clean-water insects cannot survive. Then, as temperatures fall and light levels lessen in autumn, the blanket-weed dies and partly rotted particles get washed into the gravel. Decomposition of blanket-weed can result in oxygen levels falling in salmon redds.

c) Insecticide sheep-dips
Sheep-dip that escapes into rivers kills all aquatic insect life, which is the food of fry and parr. There is evidence that the newer pyrethroid insecticides which have largely replaced organo-phosphates (as being safer for human farm workers) are particularly deadly to insects, even in tiny residual concentrations.

Sewage treatment outfalls

Even well-treated sewage has a similar effect on the river to nitrate and phosphate fertilizers. Even after treatment, the outfall will contain dissolved chemicals that are plant nutrients and encourage the growth of blanket-weed. In recent years, nitrates and phosphates present in detergents, such as washing-up liquid, have added further to the plant nutrient level of 'clean' sewage outfalls.

Scrubbers can be installed at sewage outfalls to remove nitrates and phosphates. In some parts of Europe, there are also moves to encourage (or force) farmers not to apply fertilizers to 'lanes' bordering streams and rivers. This is potentially a great step forward, for nitrate and phosphate pollution is a great 21st-century threat to clean waterways,

A cock and hen salmon pairing as an interloper looks on. The hen is not yet in spawning condition

Perfect water height conditions for running salmon are maintained for many months by the gradual release of snow–melt from the high ground. In years when little snow falls, access to the river is more difficult for the salmon

2. Physical damage to rivers

Forestry

In parts of the United States, Canada and Scandinavia, forestry has resulted in long-term damage to some salmon rivers. Logs floating downstream *en masse* have gouged out riverbeds and banks, destroying redds and nursery habitats. The wholesale removal of trees from slopes adjacent to rivers, together with the damage to the ground produced by logging vehicles, has resulted in the silting up of gravel redds and the smothering of nursery areas. On some rivers, one can still see damage that was done by logging a century ago.

Land drainage

Schemes designed to drain land adjacent to rivers and to prevent flooding have resulted in rainfall reaching the river far more quickly than before. In consequence, while spates tend to be of shorter duration, they are more violent and carry far more suspended material than in the past. Shingle banks are now more liable to movement, resulting in the destruction of redds, and even where redds are not washed away, eggs in the gravel are more likely to be suffocated through siltation.

Damage to river banks by livestock

Livestock damage has become a major problem, especially in the last fifty years because of higher stocking densities. River banks have been eroded, resulting in rivers becoming wider and, consequently, shallower. On the River Irt in north west England, some sections of the river have doubled in width since 1950 as a result of damage by livestock. Parr nurseries have been destroyed and some former gravels are no longer used as redds. Rivers that have suffered damage in this way can repair themselves if they are fenced off, and sheep and cattle are kept away from the banks.

Damming

Rivers are dammed for hydroelectricity generation or to create water-supply reservoirs. Damming of rivers has been one of the main factors in exterminating salmon populations. It caused the demise of salmon in several rivers in the United States, Sweden and Finland, and severely reduced the populations in some rivers in Ireland and France. Currently, much work is being carried out on developing systems such as fish-passes and lifts to help salmon surmount these obstacles.

> *'I should place the Erne, at Ballyshannon, as now the first river, for salmon fishing from the banks with a rod, in the British dominions.'*
>
> Sir Humphrey Davy,
> *Salmonia: or days of fly fishing*, 1828.

Not now it isn't! A hydroelectric dam was built on the Erne in the 1950s, just upstream of the town of Ballyshannon. It drowned the best lies in this short river and almost exterminated the stocks of salmon, despite the dam having a fish-pass.

Water abstraction

Abstraction is a big problem for rivers flowing close to large conurbations. It is just so easy to pipe relatively clean river water straight to a storage reservoir, then through a treatment plant and on to the consumer. The River Hodder, in north west England, is typical. Three of its main tributaries have abstraction points. In times of drought, they take so much water that over 25km (15 miles) of what should be parr nursery become almost dry. Along the main river vast areas of gravel that should have water flowing over them are exposed. Conurbations must have water, but water abstraction should be 'environmentally friendly'. Abstraction points should be low down a river system so that the entire river habitat can benefit from the water, as well as the human population. What is especially galling is that, in Britain at least, more than a quarter of the water collected for supply never reaches the consumer. It is lost in leaking pipework. And a significant part of what does reach consumers is used profligately. Wastage by consumers could be greatly reduced if all households had water meters and people had to pay for the quantity of water they used.

Salmon farming and its effects on wild salmon stocks

In 2001, the World Wild Fund for Nature (WWF) published a report, *The Status of the Atlantic Salmon, a river-by-river approach*. This report noted that, of 50 'salmon rivers' in the United States, the species had become extinct in 42 and, in the other eight, populations were at a dangerously low level. Of 32 Canadian rivers flowing into the Bay of Fundy, the WWF reported that runs were a shadow of what they had been in the 1950s. This sad state of affairs had arisen despite efforts to improve river habitat and control catches. Elsewhere in Canada, salmon runs were far healthier. The clue to the problem was that smolts leaving US rivers and rivers flowing into the Bay of Fundy had to swim through the two major centres of the salmon-farming industry. These had an annual worth (in year 2000 figures) of $60 million in the US and $220 million in Canada. Unemployment is high in the salmon-farming areas of both countries.

Salmon farming around the coast of Scotland is based mainly in sea lochs in the economically-depressed west coast, the Hebrides and Shetland. About 6,500 people are employed in the business, generating (in 2000) £300 million per annum and comprising 40% of Scottish food exports and 25% of all fish products purchased by UK consumers.

A study of rivers flowing to the west Scottish coast close to fish-farms found that these rivers had 60-82% fewer fry and 44-66% fewer parr than similar rivers not entering the sea close to fish-farms. Moreover, 86% of the smolt run from rivers entering the sea close to fish-farms was lost as it entered the sea, compared with around 26% of the smolt run entering the sea away from fish-farms. Of 28 Scottish west coast rivers studied, 14 had 'severe stock collapses' and in these about 10% of adult salmon caught were farm escapees (54% in the River Polla). In rivers flowing into the sea away from fish-farms, only 2% of salmon caught were escapees. Cross-breeding of wild and farm escapees has been shown to result in lower survival rates than in pure wild populations (see pages 128-129).

Salmon farms produce over 95% of all sea louse larvae occurring in inshore waters off western Scotland. Anglers have traditionally welcomed the sight of a couple of sea lice on the flanks of a salmon they have just caught, for they indicate that the fish has come recently from the sea. However, one Norwegian study indicated that eleven or more sea lice on the body of a smolt were likely to result in the fish dying. Another Norwegian study concluded that sea louse infestation can result in 95% smolt mortality if they have to pass close to fish farms on their way out to sea.

In Ireland, where a definite link has been established between the collapse of sea trout stocks and salmon farming, a study found that 55 sea lice on the body of a 1lb 12oz (80g) sea trout smolt results in physiological stress; reduced haemoglobin and difficulty in controlling salt concentrations in the body fluids. It was found that in those bays in the west of Ireland that have salmon farms, 38% of smolts had above stress-level numbers of sea lice. In bays lacking salmon farms, only 3.4% of smolts had critical sea louse infestation.

Under the European Union Habitats & Birds Directive, the British and Irish governments and the Scottish Parliament have an obligation to conserve salmon stocks. By having no statutory regulations on the location and operation of salmon farms, these governments are failing in their duty.

Farmed salmon are defined by
their dense spotting, ragged
fins and portly shape

Damage to wild salmon stocks by escaped farmed salmon

Although they are the same species as wild salmon, farmed salmon are genetically rather different. They have been selectively bred over several generations for a quick growth rate and a tolerance of living together in overcrowded cages. Wild, genetically-controlled traits have been bred out of them.

Unfortunately, security of cages in salmon farms is nowhere near 100%, even in sheltered sea inlets. Heavy seas destroy cages. Seals bite through the cage netting to get to the salmon. Every year, large numbers escape. There have even been reports of salmon-farmers releasing surplus stock on purpose. In 1989-91, 40% of the commercial catch from the ocean feeding ground north of the Faroes consisted of farm escapees. Subsequent figures are closer to 20%, and most originated from Norwegian salmon farms. Today, there are escaped farm salmon running upstream and spawning with the wild stock in just about every river around the western coast of Ireland, in Scotland from the Solway to Moray Firths, and in southern and western Norway. Anglers and fishery scientists have protested, believing that this crossbreeding was likely to affect wild salmon stocks.

Eleven scientists in Ireland pooled their expertise to research the problem. The work was carried out at Burrishoole. Here it was possible not only to generate experimental genetic crosses, but also to catch every smolt produced as it headed out to sea and every salmon that returned. By DNA analysis, it was possible to identify the parents of each adult salmon recaptured. The crosses made were: wild x wild, farmed x farmed, wild x farmed (the progeny of this cross were known as F1), F1 x F1, wild x F1 and farmed x F1. The progeny of each cross were raised to eyed-ova stage and then released into streams devoid of any wild salmon. The results were first described at a conference held in Edinburgh in 2002, *Salmon at the Edge* (Mills 2003).

The Burrishoole results concluded that escaped farmed salmon breeding with wild salmon constituted a major threat to the genetic integrity, survival and production of the wild fish. The parr of farmed salmon and of crosses with farmed salmon grew more rapidly than wild parr and ousted wild parr from the experimental river. However, overall survival to smolt stage of all crosses that included any farmed fish genes were much lower than for wild x wild fish. Consequently, in a healthy river

with a maximum stock of parr, introduction of farmed or hybrid fish will lower smolt production.

A much larger proportion of wild smolts returned as adult salmon than did farmed x farmed smolts (7.9% compared with 0.3%), and the majority were one-sea-winter grilse. All other progeny that had farmed blood had a lower return rate of adults than did wild x wild smolts. Interestingly, though the numbers were small, the F1 x F1 cross generated the highest proportion of 2SW returns.

The researchers concluded that when farmed and hybrid salmon occur in a river, the result will be a reduction in the number of adults returning and, "*since reduction is cumulative, repeated introductions [of farm escapees] in a population on the verge of self-sustainability, could result in an extinction vortex.*"

Previously, riverkeepers killed everything with curved beaks and talons. They also killed mergansers and cormorants. It is now recognised that the diver family, including this Black-throated Diver, have no effect whatsoever on salmon stocks

The importance of single river management

If the Atlantic salmon as a species was in danger of extinction, all commercial and rod-and-line fishing should be stopped until the population had recovered and the species was no longer endangered. The truth is, however, that salmon are not endangered.

What of rivers where salmon stocks are abysmally low, perhaps because the river habitat has been degraded (see pages 118-121) The first answer is to stop commercial fishing. What about angling? Should not rod-and-line fishing also be stopped until the population of that particular river has recovered? There is actually no need to impose a moratorium on angling. Indeed, to stop rod-and-line fishing might even add to the problem.

If angling is stopped on a particular river, the income derived from angling disappears. Not only does the local economy suffer, but the income that pays for bailiffs and river-keepers goes too. If that happens, the few remaining salmon in the river lose the protection of those whose livelihoods depend on the survival of the fish. Furthermore, anglers themselves have a prime interest in the prosperity of their quarry. No-one gives the future of the salmon greater priority than the salmon angler.

Where a river's salmon population is causing concern, it is essential that fishery owners, scientists, government fishery bodies and anglers co-operate to improve the salmon runs. Research may be needed to determine why the stocks are low. There may be pollution that must be identified and rectified, or dams that need fish-passes, or redds that are silting up too easily, or poor parr habitat. Many rivers still have excellent runs of salmon, despite the increase in mortality out in the Atlantic that has occurred at the end of the 20th century. Any river that does not have a reasonable run of salmon has some inherent problem(s). If this (or these) can be identified and rectified, the salmon will do the rest themselves.

It is important, however, that salmon anglers appreciate their responsibility to salmon conservation, by adhering to bag limits and following catch-and-release policies (see page 127).

That single river management schemes are successful can be gauged from work done on the Loire-Allier by the Fondation Saumon. In Britain, with its dense human population, and the most intensively-farmed countryside in the world, concerns for the salmon have led to organisations such as the Tweed and Eden Foundations. Even smaller rivers, such as the Lune and Ribble, often have their own conservation trusts. These organisations exist because of anglers who fish for salmon.

Catch-and-release as a management tool

'But salmon and trout play so important a part in the lives of many of us, they are so interwoven with our happiest days, with our hopes, our joys, our fears, our sorrows, that we can never be satisfied.'

G.H. Nall, *The Life of the Sea Trout*, 1930

There is no evidence that rod-and-line fishing has ever threatened the stocks of wild salmon in any river. However, when stocks in a river are low every salmon is precious and should be encouraged to run upstream to spawn. In these instances, catch-and-release is important.

Catch-and-release is a relatively recent river management tool. It was first used on Nova Scotia's Margaree River in 1979. The first totally catch-and-release rivers were the Big Salmon River and three headwaters of the Miramichi (New Brunswick) in 1981. By 1984, Canada's Department of Fisheries and Oceans introduced some level of catch-and-release to all of their Atlantic salmon rivers.

Research carried out on the Aberdeenshire Dee and the River Tay in Scotland has shown that there can be nearly 100% survival in released rod-caught salmon, provided the job is done properly. This is backed up by the experience and observations of salmon rod fisheries in many other parts of the world.

Good catch-and-release practice

1. Attitude of Mind
'If I'm going to release this salmon that has just taken my fly, does it really matter if it gets off before I land it?' For most anglers, it is the deception of the fish and the 'take' that are important.

2. Use barbless single hooks
Barbless hooks are very easy to slip out of the jaw of a fish. In practice, barbless single hooks lose surprisingly few fish, compared with barbed double and treble hooks. But bear in mind the first point made here.

3. Use adequately strong tackle
If one uses strong tackle, fish can be landed more quickly and therefore returned in a stronger condition than if lighter tackle had been used. Get the fish in as quickly as you can, but if the hook happens to pull out, bear in mind the first point made here.

4. Never, ever lift a salmon that you want to release from the water.
Lifting a heavy fish from the water can cause damage to internal organs. Lifting a heavy fish by the tail can damage the vertebral column and/or musculature and internal organs. Instead, use a large submerged landing net, with knotless mesh.

Remove the hook with the fish still in the water. If one then takes the net away and holds the fish gently around the 'wrist' of the tail, it can be supported with its head into the current until it regains its strength and can swim away strongly. If you want a photograph, keep the fish in the water surface and well supported. When an exhausted salmon is held out of the water, its gills collapse. It can no longer breathe and its chances of survival are reduced by the second.

Some anglers are opposed to the concept of catch-and-release. They are entitled to their opinion. They would not, of course, fish a river where catch-and-release is a management tool.

In 1997, the statistics for catch-and-release of salmon caught on rod and line in various countries were as follow: USA ca. 100%; Russia ca. 87%; Canada ca. 51%; England and Wales ca. 23%; Scotland ca. 18%; Iceland ca. 5%.

The hatchery as a management tool

The first salmon hatchery was set up on the River Rhine in 1852. Since then, fish hatcheries have proliferated around the world. Wild salmon should always be used as the brood-stock. Farmed salmon strains which may have had certain wild characteristics bred out of them should never be used. Fish are taken from the river when almost ready to spawn. The eggs and milt are carefully stripped from the hen and cock fish respectively. Fertilization takes place in a bowl or bucket and the spent adults are returned to the river.

The 'green' eggs are taken into the hatchery where they may be incubated in running water to the 'eyed-ova' stage. They may then be put out into the river even at this early stage of development. Alternatively, they may be kept in the hatchery while development continues (through alevin) to the 'unfed fry' or 'fed fry' stage and then released. Young salmon may also be kept in enclosures and reared to the smolt stage before release into the river to migrate downstream to the sea. The earlier in the development sequence that the fish are put out into the river, the less the cost.

Set against this, the mortality of very young fish (between the eyed-ova and smolt stages) is much lower in the protected environment of the hatchery. In some cases, hatcheries produce more smolts than the rivers they serve can produce naturally. It has been shown, however, that salmon that have been raised in a hatchery and released as smolts have a much lower survival rate than wild smolts, or those that have grown in the river from stocked eyed-ova or fry. Recently, it has been shown that hatchery smolt survival can be increased slightly if the smolts are first conditioned to life in the wild by releasing them into smolt-ponds. These are enclosed pools in which the smolts can be 'hardened-off', where they can experience spates, sand and silt in the water and get used to taking some wild food, before they are fully released.

There are two valid reasons for using a hatchery as part of river management.

1. To restore a salmon run in a river that has lost all its salmon stock due to pollution or some other catastrophe. Eventually, this should result in a self-regenerating wild population, at which point the hatchery becomes redundant. When the Tyne estuary was first cleaned up in the 1980s and the river was once more capable of supporting a thriving salmon population, the hatchery output contributed up to 35% of the annual run. By 2003, however, the hatchery was no longer necessary. If a river can produce naturally its optimum number of smolts, the use of a hatchery is a waste of money.
2. To compensate for the loss of important stretches of river through damming. Many Swedish rivers draining into the Baltic lost their salmon stocks through the building of hydroelectric dams, which eliminated the spawning headwaters. In order to make up for the loss of spawning grounds, hatcheries were established to produce smolts for these rivers. These smolts go out to sea and return to the river in which they were released as mature salmon. Since, however, these returning salmon have nowhere to go to reproduce, as many as possible are caught and their spawn and milt harvested for the next hatchery generation of smolts. It has been estimated that over half the present day Baltic salmon population originated from hatcheries. This practice of releasing smolts and harvesting all that return is known as salmon ranching.

Salmon ranching is also carried out on some rivers which naturally have very poor spawning and nursery areas (e.g. the Ranga in Iceland), or to enhance sparse wild runs (e.g. the Delphi in Ireland).

...and the future?

Provided we continue to improve the quality of salmon rivers, as has been done over the last two or three decades, the future of the Atlantic salmon lies in the Atlantic Ocean itself. There are three possible scenarios:

1. The oceanic climate continues in its present state. If this occurs, salmon mortality at sea will remain fairly high, especially for fish that would otherwise have returned as MSW salmon. Our efforts to improve the fresh water habitat will result in improved smolt production in rivers. If governments can be persuaded to regulate the salmon farming industry (to reduce sea louse infestations and escapees), we will see runs increase in some rivers and reduced genetic contamination of wild salmon populations.

2. The oceanic climate improves. If this happens, salmon survival at sea could improve dramatically and match that of the 1960s. If, as well as this, we continued to improve river habitats, and if the problems associated with salmon farming can be addressed, salmon populations could flourish as they have not done in recent history.

3. The oceanic climate worsens. Were this to occur, *Salmo salar* could easily become extinct – everywhere.

If the third of these scenarios were to become a reality, I wouldn't hold out much hope for *Homo sapiens* either! But I am an optimist.

Bibliography & Further Reading

Books marked * are recommended reading.
Those marked ** are collections of papers from scientific conferences.

BEETON, Mrs. Isabella, Beeton's Book of Household Management, The Englishwoman's Domestic Magazine, London 1859-61

BERNERS, Dame Juliana (attrib.), Treatyse of Fysshynge with an Angle, Westminster Press, London 1496

From The Boke of St. Albans, Wynkyn de Woorde

BOYLAN, P. et al. (eds.), Seals/Atlantic Salmon Interaction Workshop, Loughs Agency, Londonderry, nd [2004]*

BUCKLAND, Frank, Familiar History of British Fishes, SPCK, London 1873

CHAPMAN, Abel, The Borders and Beyond, Gurney & Jackson, London & Edinburgh 1924

CHOLMONDELEY-PENNELL, H. Fishing: Salmon and Trout, The Badminton Library, Longmans, Grant & Co., London 1885

COLQUHOUN, John, The Moor and the Loch (6th edn.), Blackwood, Edinburgh & London 1886

DAVY, Sir Humphrey, Salmonia or days of fly fishing, John Murray, London 1828

DARWIN, Charles, The Origin of Species, John Murray, London 1859

FAHY, Edward, Child of the Tides, Glendale Press, Dun Laoghaire 1985

FALKUS, Hugh, Salmon Fishing, HF & G Witherby, London 1984

FISHERIES CONSERVANCY BOARD FOR NORTHERN IRELAND, Annual Reports

FRANCIS, Francis, A Book of Angling (5th edn.), Herbert Jenkins, London 1920

FRESHWATER FISHERIES LABORATORY, Annual and Biennial Reviews, Department of Agriculture and Fisheries for Scotland/Scottish Executive*

GREY OF FALLODEN, Lord, Fly Fishing, Temple Press, Letchworth 1930

HARDY, Sir Alister, The Open Sea: Its Natural History. Fish & Fisheries, Collins 'New Naturalist', London 1959*

HARDY, Sir Alister, The Open Sea: Its Natural History. The World of Plankton, Collins 'New Naturalist', London 1957*

HOUGHTON, Revd. W., British Fresh-Water Fishes, Peerage Books, London 1984 (facsimile)

HOWLETT, Robert, The Angler's Sure Guide, London 1706

JENKINS, J. Travis, The Fishes of the British Isles, Frederick Warne, London 1925

JONES, J.W., The Atlantic Salmon, Collins 'New Naturalist', London 1959*

MILLS, Derek, Ecology and Management of Atlantic Salmon, Chapman & Hall, London 1989*

MILLS, Derek, Salmon and Trout: A resource, its ecology, conservation and management, Oliver & Boyd, Edinburgh 1971*

MILLS, Derek (ed.), Salmon at the Edge, Blackwell Science, Oxford 2003**

MILLS, Derek and PIGGINS, David (eds.), Atlantic Salmon: Planning for the Future, Croome Helm, London & Sydney 1988**

NALL, G.A., The Sea Trout, Seeley Service, London 1930*

NETBOY, Anthony, The Salmon: their fight for survival, (Houghton Mifflin), Faber 1974

NETBOY, Anthony, Salmon: the World's most harassed fish, Andre Deutsch, London 1980*

O'GORMAN, The Practice of Angling, William Curry, Dublin 1845

RIGHYNI, R., Salmon Taking Times MacDonald, London 1965

SCROPE, William, Days & Nights Salmon Fishing John Murray, London 1843

SEELEY, H.G., The Fresh-Water Fishes of Europe, Cassell, London 1886

SHEARER, W.M., The Atlantic Salmon, Fishing News Books, Oxford 1992*

SMITH, M.W., and CARTER, W.M. (eds.), International Atlantic Salmon Symposium, International Salmon Foundation 1972**

TOLFRY, Frederick, Jones's Guide to Norway, Longman, London 1848

TRAHERNE, John P., Habits of the Salmon, Chapman & Hall, London, 1889

VENABLES, Col. Robert, The Experienced Angler, Richard Marriot, London 1662

WADDINGTON, Richard, Salmon Fishing, Faber, London 1959

WALTON, Izaak, The Compleat Angler (5th edn.), London 1676

WHEELER, Alwyne, The Fishes of the British Isles and N.W. Europe, Macmillan, London 1969

WHORISKEY, F.G., and WELAN, K.E. (eds.), Managing Wild Atlantic Salmon, Vth International Atlantic Salmon Symposium 1997**

WULFF, Lee, The Atlantic Salmon, Winchester Press, Piscataway, NJ 1958

YARRELL, William, A History of British Fishes, Van Vorst, London 1836

Index

Glossary

Ovum (plural: Ova) The egg   2, 21, 24, 28, 73, 128

Milt The fluid released at spawning time by the male. Milt contains the sperm that fertilises the ova   21, 24, 26

Redd The gravel in which the female salmon lays her eggs   24

Eyed-ovum The egg showing the eyes of developing fish as two black spots   28

Alevin The newly-hatched young salmon, still in the redd, and still receiving nourishment from its large yolk sac   2, 29, 30, 41

Fry The young salmon after the yolk sac becomes exhausted and before it gains its parr marks (see below) and takes up its own territory   2, 29-32, 43, 122, 128

Fed-fry The fry that has swum up from the gravel of its redd and begun to feed

Parr The stage at which the juvenile salmon does most of its feeding in freshwater   2, 26-46, 62, 78, 82, 106, 122

Parr marks Oval grey markings, often likened to finger-prints, which are found down the side of the parr   29

Precocious parr Parr as they become sexually mature   26

Smolt Silver juvenile salmon that are heading downstream to the sea   2, 23, 30, 36-38, 45-50, 62, 73, 78, 82, 106, 122, 128-129

Post-smolt A salmon that is feeding at sea   2, 50-61, 79, 90

Grilse = 1 Sea Winter (1SW) salmon. A salmon that returns to its river to spawn after one winter (plus the months on either side of that winter) feeding at sea   2, 61, 64, 81, 86, 88, 92, 96-97

Salmon, including: 2 Sea Winter (2SW), 3 Sea Winter (3SW), 4 Sea Winter (4SW) and Multi Sea Winter (MSW) salmon. The term 'salmon' refers to fish that remain out at sea, feeding and growing, for at least a year longer than the grilse (see above)   2, 21-26, 52-54, 62, 68-102

Repeat spawner A fish that has spawned, headed back to sea to feed and recover, and then returned to spawn for a second or third time   84-85, 102-103

Kelt A salmon that has spawned, but not yet returned to sea to feed and recover   2, 23, 80-81, 85, 102-103

Mended kelt A kelt that is (or appears to be) recovering from the rigours of spawning

Baggot A hen salmon that has failed to lay her eggs   26

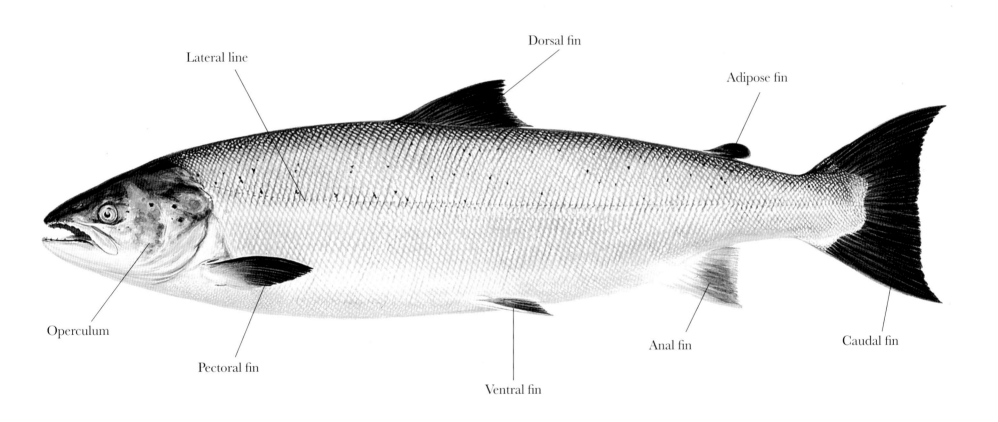

Lateral line

Dorsal fin

Adipose fin

Operculum

Pectoral fin

Ventral fin

Anal fin

Caudal fin

Acknowledgements

This book is not a scientific textbook so, though it contains a distillation of conference reports, papers and other texts, some conventions have been abandoned. There are no '(Bloggs, 2006)' scattered through the text, nor are there statistical data (e.g. p<0.001), algebraic formulae, complex tables or graphs to distract non-scientific readers. Here, then, are acknowledged those whose sterling work and writings on salmon have been consulted; major works are listed in References and Further Reading (p. 130).

Our thanks to: J. Anderson, J.D. Armstrong, J. Arrignon, G.R. Bigg, J. Browne, D.K. Cairns, E.M.P. Chadwick, S. Chase, R.G. Crawford, R. Cuinat, R. Doughty, K.F. Drinkwater, P.F Elson, J.H. Fenety, Andrew Ferguson, J.E. Greer, Thor Gudjonsson, S.H.I. Jakupsstovn, J.M. Jensen, R.A. Jones, L.P. Hansen, A.D. Hawkins, M. Holm, J.C. Holst, S. Hughes, J.A. Jacobsen, P. Jakobsen, G.J.A. Kennedy, G.L. Lacroix, G.C. de Leaniz, P. McGinnity, J.J. Martinez, G.W. Mawle, S.J. Middlemas, N.J. Milner, Derek Mills, W.A. Montevecchi, D. Moor, C.C. Mullins, F. Nilsen, D.J. Piggins, D.G. Reddin, Jeremy Reed, W.M. Shearer, J. Sturlaugsson, W.R. Turrell, J.A.M. Ventura, John Webb, H.C. White, A. Whitehead and F.G. Whoriskey.

Our especial thanks to Patrick Martin of the Fondation Saumon, Richard (Dick) Shelton, Ross Gardiner and the staff at the Freshwater Fisheries Laboratory (Pitlochry, Scotland), the Freshwater Biological Association, and to John Todd and The Foyle Fisheries Commission.

Also to Peter Grey, Ralph Northumberland, Paul Morgan (Cochy Bonddu Books), Jo Dovey, Zane Foster and Ivan Swaile.

Useful Organisations

Atlantic Salmon Trust
Moulin
Pitlochry
Perthshire
PH26 5JQ
Scotland
Tel: 01796 473439
Fax: 01796 473554
email: director@atlanticsalmon
trust.org

Atlantic Salmon Federation
P.O. Box 5200
St. Andrews
New Brunswick E5B 3S8
or
P.O. Box 807
Calais
Maine 04619-0807
Canada
U.S.A.
Tel: 506 529-4581
email: asf@nbnet.nb.ca
website: www.asf.ca

Salmon & Trout Association
Fishmongers' Hall
London Bridge
London EC4R 9EL
England
Tel: 020 7283 5838
Fax: 020 7626 5137
Email: hq@salmon-trout.org
Website: www.salmon-trout.org

Association pour
la Fondation Saumon
Salmoniculture du Haut-Allier
Chanteuges
43300 Langeac
France
Tél : + 33 (0)4 71 74 05 45
Fax : + 33 (0)4 71 74 05 44
email : info@fondation-
saumon.org

North Atlantic Salmon Fund
(NASF)
Skipholti 35
105 Reykjavik
Iceland
email: nasf@vortex.is